PSYCHOLOGY & THE SOLDIER

PSYCHOLOGY AND
THE SOLDIER

BY

F. C. BARTLETT, M.A.

*Fellow of St John's College Cambridge,
Reader in Experimental Psychology
and Director of the Psychological
Laboratory of the University
of Cambridge*

CAMBRIDGE
AT THE UNIVERSITY PRESS
MCMXXVII

CAMBRIDGE
UNIVERSITY PRESS

University Printing House, Cambridge CB2 8BS, United Kingdom

Cambridge University Press is part of the University of Cambridge.

It furthers the University's mission by disseminating knowledge in the pursuit of
education, learning and research at the highest international levels of excellence.

www.cambridge.org
Information on this title: www.cambridge.org/9781107455603

© Cambridge University Press 1927

First published 1927
First paperback edition 2014

A catalogue record for this publication is available from the British Library

ISBN 978-1-107-45560-3 Paperback

PREFACE

During the Great War of 1914—1918 every important belligerent country called upon its psychologists for technical advice and assistance, and by common consent much of the work done proved of the greatest value. When the War was over and courses of Military Study were being re-organised in Cambridge, lectures dealing with psychology in relation to military problems were begun. They were due to the initiative of Dr C. S. Myers, C.B.E., F.R.S., who was then Director of the Cambridge Psychological Laboratory, and who had been Official Psychologist to the British Expeditionary Force in France, and Lieut.-Col. L. H. Thornton, C.M.G., D.S.O., who was then Director of Military Studies at Cambridge. These lectures have been continued since that time, and I have been responsible for them for the last six years. The present book is a selection from the lectures delivered in connexion with this Course. It does not in any way pretend to be a complete treatment of the relations of Psychology to the soldier and to his life. It is merely an introduction to an important field of applied psychology which has in the past been unduly neglected.

I am very greatly indebted to Brig.-Gen. E. W. Costello, V.C., C.M.G., C.V.O., D.S.O., Director of Military Studies at the University of Cambridge, for his encouragement and help in the production of this small volume. He read through the whole of the typescript and made a number of exceedingly valuable comments and criticisms, many, though not all of which, I have most gladly accepted. It will be obvious to every reader that some of the questions discussed, particularly in Part II, are of a controversial character, and for the opinions expressed or adopted therein I must accept all responsibility.

I should also like to say that the plan and mode of discussion have gained greatly from the criticisms and difficulties freely expressed by many students during the years of my lectures. To them, also, I am grateful.

That the treatment is, as a whole, expressed in general terms and may often appear somewhat theoretical is inevitable in a book of the present size, or, indeed, of any size short of a series of large volumes. There is no need to remind the soldier that every man must learn for himself how to apply that modification of general principles which will solve specific practical problems.

F. C. BARTLETT

CAMBRIDGE,
September 24, 1927

CONTENTS

CONTENTS

PART THREE
MENTAL DISORDERS OF WARFARE

GENERAL INTRODUCTION

IF THE DUKE OF WELLINGTON had been accused
of being a psychologist, his reply would probably
have been brief but very emphatic. On one occa-
sion, however, he was trying to state the qualities
of a great captain. "One must understand," he
remarked, "the mechanism and power of the individual soldier, then that of a company, or battalion, or brigade, and so on, before one can venture
to group divisions or move an army." Personal
courage is necessary and valuable, but is by itself
utterly inadequate. In discussing Sir John Moore,
Wellington said: "He was as brave as his own
sword, but he did not know what men could do
or could not do."[1]

There, in a nutshell, is the case for the application
of psychological study to the problems of building
and training an army. For it is the psychologist's
business to try to understand "the mechanism and
power" of the individual, to know "what men can
do and what they cannot do," and to learn how
human conduct is governed.

A modern army is an immense and complicated
organisation demanding highly specialised skill
and knowledge in many of its branches. In recent
years it has advanced towards mechanisation in all
directions. Yet it still depends ultimately for its
success upon the degree of insight and under-

[1] W. H. Fitchett: *The Great Duke*, London 1911, x.

standing with which the men who compose it are treated. Mechanical transport, modern artillery, tanks, aeroplanes, wireless apparatus, gas warfare, technical methods for the detection of enemy guns, aeroplanes, and submarines—in fact all the numerous applications of physics, chemistry, and engineering are at the mercy of the human mechanism by which they are employed. It is the task of the psychologist to attempt to understand that mechanism. And even though at present he can fulfil his task only partially, yet the knowledge that he has gained is important to all those who, in any practical endeavour, have to deal with men either as individuals or in the mass.

Psychology has undergone a very great change during recent years. It is no longer merely a matter of the study, but of the laboratory and of daily life. Not long ago psychologists were chiefly concerned to give a detailed description of the contents of the human mind and of the ways in which the structure of our knowledge is built up. If a man turns away for a time from the things of the outside world and tries to attend to his own mental life, he discovers *sensations* which arise when he sees colours, hears sounds, touches or tastes objects and so on; *images* when he allows himself to dwell upon the events of his past life which are no longer present in his immediate outward surroundings; and *ideas* when he is concerned with general relations and qualities that are treated as independent of merely particular instances. These do not simply lie about in his mind in a disorderly fashion. They are tied or organised together, built up into various groups. Whenever a man thinks, each has its special place and all have their own parts to play. Confronted by some particular external situation to which he must somehow adapt himself, he learns a little about the situation through the activity of his special senses. What he learns may arouse images of other situations or of fragments of other situations, like to or different from the one now before him. These combining, changing, developing may enable him to separate the accidents of the present from its essential features, and he may arrive at some formulation in general terms of what the situation means, or he may adopt what he calls a reasoned plan of action. Now if all this happens to a man who has the right sort of mind and who has a fair amount of leisure, he may begin to speculate about the nature of all the various factors which are involved. What *is* a sensation? What *is* an image? What *is* an idea? he may ask. To answer these questions he delves once more into the recesses of his own mental life, and tries to describe what all of them seem to be like when he experiences them, how in the course of experience they all get linked together, and how far the knowledge which he gains by their means can be accepted as genuine. He may call the result "psychology"; but however successful he may be in his attempt, his answers do not throw much light, and are not of course intended to throw much light upon his conduct when sensations, images, and ideas occur to him. Whatever may be the exact nature of the sensations of sound as actual experiences, for example, the hungry man, when he hears the dinner bell, will hurry to the dining-room, while the man who is not hungry may continue whatever he is doing till the latest possible moment, and then be moved, very likely, to a violent protest.

Consequently speculations about the exact nature of the contents of mind have tended to give place more and more to a study of how people behave, and why they behave as they do. The psychologist is no longer wrapped up in himself. Looking out into the world, he naturally is at once struck by the amazing variety of things that men do. He wants to find out why one man does this thing and another that, and why one man does this well and another the same thing ill. At once he is a step nearer to experiment. For he can contrive to make a man do things, and in this way learn about the conditions of such action. Psychology is now less preoccupied with an analysis and description of the materials and structure of knowledge, and very much more with a study of the conditions of all forms of human and animal behaviour. The psychologist must push into all the fields of man's activity, both normal and abnormal, and particularly into all those fields where human activity is most definitely organised and regulated. He is therefore bound to be interested in the Army, and if his interest leads to any insight, the Army must in return be interested in him.

Psychology may, then, be defined as *a systematic attempt to understand the conditions of human activity*. The term "activity," as it is used here, must be given a somewhat generous interpretation. The external circumstances of two people may be very much the same; their bodily attitudes may be very similar. But we cannot, by studying the external circumstances and by observing, however accurately, the bodily attitudes, say exactly what they are thinking about. Yet their thinking must be regarded as a form of activity. A dream is a form of activity. Having an image is a form of activity. There are in fact many forms or instances of activity which only the person who displays them can tell us about. Not only so, but it is evident that what a person thinks may have no small influence upon some of his more obvious forms of behaviour both then and later. For much of our evidence concerning the conditions of activity we are driven to go to the person whose behaviour we are studying and to rely upon what he can tell us. Whether this must render many of the psychological formulations of the conditions of activity finally uncertain, since a man is very liable to error in the matter of his own inner life, I do not now propose to discuss. The fact must be admitted, and instead of discussing its exact significance in general terms, it is better to see what psychology, in spite of this difficulty, is able to accomplish.

5

Sometimes people say that psychology should consider *only* that type of condition which has to be expressed in terms of a man's own inner experience. But this is a needlessly impossible position. Suppose a group of men who are fighting have to meet a gas attack launched by the enemy. Their conduct depends in the most direct manner upon the physical and chemical constitution of the gases which they have to meet, and upon the respiratory and other changes which those physical and chemical conditions may set up in their bodies. It depends also upon the group's *morale*, upon the individual's timidity or daring, upon the leader's insight and skill. To ignore the physical and physiological conditions will produce as faulty and fragmentary an understanding of their conduct as to overlook those conditions which belong more immediately or exclusively to the mental and social make-up of the persons concerned. In studying the conditions which determine human activity the psychologist must consider:

(*a*) the physical conditions, i.e. those which belong to a man's external environment;

(*b*) the physiological conditions, i.e. those which belong to a man's bodily organism; and

(*c*) those other conditions which belong to the man's own life, but which so far nobody has succeeded in expressing adequately in physical or physiological terms. For example, a groom may be fearless with a horse, a *shikari* with a wounded tiger or on bad ground, and yet both may be cowards in other circumstances. This third group of conditions are what are generally termed psychological. But the psychologist is by no means called upon to shut himself up in the study of these alone.

We must now turn once more to the modern army and try to realise some of the important problems which confront its makers. On the one hand an army is like an immensely complicated machine possessing many delicate and highly specialised parts. On the other hand it is based upon some of the most simple, fundamental, and unspecialised of all human tendencies. Any one of its technical branches depends for its success upon the possession by those who man it of specialised abilities which have been trained in the best possible way to the completest possible efficiency. Take the enormous development in recent years of mechanicalised transport. The growth of this depends upon the practical application of scientific discoveries of a very technical nature. The use of it demands men who have specialised knowledge and specialised interests. It is impossible to say of any group of men, taken haphazard, that each member of that group is just as likely as any other to be able to understand and apt to apply the special knowledge and behaviour which any branch of mechanical transport demands. A successful man may need special visual skill, particular forms of manual dexterity and muscular control, the sort of imagery that is able to cope with mechanical problems; and these must all be backed up by interests which turn naturally in the direction of the management of swift forms of locomotion. The same kind of thing is true of each arm of a modern signalling service. Here again special problems demand special capacities: a high standard of keeness of vision, in some instances accurate colour discrimination, in others well developed acoustic capacities, so that particular sounds may be immediately recognised and accurately localised. Similarly in regard to every technical branch of an army, special demand is made upon some fundamental sensory reaction, such as particular skill in vision, hearing, touch, or control of bodily movement; upon the possession of some predominant type of concrete imagery; upon a special temperamental quality or combination of temperamental qualities; upon a particular acquisition of knowledge. It may seem that the last of these, the possession of specialised knowledge, is merely a matter of teaching. But a man does not learn simply what he is told. He learns only that part of what he is told in which he is interested; and interests are less easily made to order than has been popularly or officially supposed.

Now all these types of human activity are exactly the concern of the more technical part of present-day psychology. They are what the psychologist studies in his laboratory. It is his business to know how the eye, the ear, the skin, the muscles react when certain specific conditions are provided. He has developed his own technique for testing, ranking, understanding these reactions. He deals similarly with the common kinds of imagery, and with special types of memory. He is beginning to work out his own ways of discovering temperamental capacities, and so of understanding and controlling their expression. This is laboratory work which has an immediate application to a large number of problems of military organisation.

But no matter how highly technical may be his immediate work, the good army man is primarily and fundamentally a fighter. I think this is true even of the more sedentary branches of the service, and it is certainly true of those whose place is in the field. Moreover it is probably still correct to say, that the success in practice of the most highly technical branches of an army depends upon the efficiency and steadfastness of the least specialised arms of all—the mass of the infantry and cavalry. Nobody would argue that the modern infantry-man is unskilled. But he requires less specialised abilities and less specialised knowledge than many of his fellows. He must have the capacity to with-stand fatigue, must possess endurance, courage, dis-cipline, loyalty, a gift of comradeship, and, unless he is to be a source of serious weakness in a crisis, a pugnacity which is not solely dependent upon group stimulation. These more general and widely spread qualities have distinguished all the great organised fighters since fighting began. The psy-chological problems here are, correspondingly, more general ones. How can these qualities be trained and developed, and kept bright and burnished and ready for use? To answer this question a knowledge of laboratory technique is of little avail. The psychologist must now go out into the world of daily events and mingle with men therein. He must try to observe the primary driving forces which build up character and conduct. And if he cannot then acquire the insight to enable him to find at any rate some part of the answer to this question for himself and others, he is a poor psychologist and his psychology is a feeble instrument.

There is a special set of problems which, in view of the nature of modern warfare, are of particular importance to the military psychologist. To the bulk of an army the modern war is a war of position rather than one of movement. In spite of the most elaborate systems of relief, according to which a man is in the front line of fighting for only relatively short periods, this subjects a soldier to a well-nigh intolerable strain. If there is any weakness in his mental character, the war of position is apt to find it out and to work upon it. Probably every character, even the most stable, will crack and break under certain conditions of prolonged strain. But some are much more liable to be upset than others. These, at a crisis, are a profound source of weakness. They not only suffer themselves, they readily and unwittingly contaminate others, for a group in a tight position is often peculiarly liable to suggestion.

In some cases it can be predicted with practical

certainty that a man will suffer mental collapse or disorder if he is subjected to the strain of trench-warfare under normal modern conditions. There are people who are mentally unfitted for certain branches of a fighting force just as there are people who are physically unsound, and the first may be discovered almost as certainly and definitely as the second. Once they are found, they should, for the purposes of the army, be eliminated from further consideration. There is no point in finding "soft billets" for the weaklings. Such a policy is not only dangerous in itself, but is disastrous in its reaction upon those who have to bear genuine hardship.

In other and far more numerous cases the risk must be taken. But then it is important for the military student, particularly for the officer, to know the commonest conditions of that mental strain which leads to actual pathological break-down, and to be able to recognise the incipient stages of such disease. By a knowledge of the first he can take all possible steps to guard against this great cause of individual and collective loss of *morale*, and by an acquaintance with the second he can often prevent individual cases from reaching acute and dangerous stages of disorder.

I have now completed this preliminary survey. In what follows I propose to take up three main groups of problems.

First, I shall try to show something of how the more technical laboratory type of psychology can help to solve the problems involved in choosing and training the recruit. Secondly, I shall show how a knowledge of social psychology, with its study of the ways in which individual activity is modified by membership of a group, may be brought to bear upon the problems of the maintenance of discipline, the functions of leadership, and the development of *morale*. Thirdly, I shall attempt to give a brief account of some of the mental disorders of warfare and of their treatment, in so far as a knowledge of these matters is necessary and helpful to the ordinary military officer.

PART ONE

CHOOSING AND TRAINING THE RECRUIT

Chapter I. THE GENERAL EXAMINATION

TESTING THE SPECIAL SENSES

It is obvious that both physiologically and psychologically not everybody is equally fitted to belong to an army. This is already almost universally admitted, and the incoming recruit is first made to undergo a general entrance examination, on the basis of which he may be either rejected or provisionally accepted. Further, the nature of the examination is usually varied according to the branch of the Service which the recruit wishes to enter, and is roughly more difficult and more specialised the more technical is the operation which he desires to undertake.

With the general physiological or "medical" examination the psychologist has, of course, no particular concern. Yet one important difference between the point of view of the ordinary doctor and that of the psychologist must be emphasised. On the whole the doctor is chiefly concerned with bodily structure, and the psychologist with function. The ordinary medical man carefully examines the way in which the body and parts of the body are made, and assumes that if these show no particular structural defects the man will be able successfully to carry out the activities of military life. But the psychologist is concerned directly with the conditions of activity, and he recognises that structural factors are only a part of those conditions. Thus, to take an illustration not in itself specifically psychological, a man may conform to high standards of bodily structure and may yet be peculiarly liable to petty illnesses, to "colds in the head," to lowered resistance to fatigue and the like, which are very irritating and may be even dangerous in any ordinary military group. The psychologist, in those parts of a general entrance examination which are his special concern, is less interested to discover the exact state of physical or mental structure at the moment of examination than to find out precisely what a man may be expected to *do* under certain assignable conditions.

A general admission examination must obviously have negative rather than positive significance. It is directed more to the elimination of the unfit than to the sorting or classification of the fit. We desire to know, however, not merely that a man is in general fit for military service, but also for what branch of military service he may be best adapted. The business of detecting specialised abilities is a very important part of modern applied psychology. The more varied and technical become the different arms of military service, the more important it is to apply to their organisation any methods which can be shown to save time and money in training and to improve the efficiency of the trained material.

At present there is undoubtedly a considerable wastage of time and money, and often no small aggravation of temper during the Recruit Training period which follows the general medical examination. Any efficient way of lessening these, by diminishing the number of men who are finally eliminated *after* training, should be warmly welcomed. There are many arguments in favour of the organisation of a Central Examining Depôt for all Arms-Branches, and this could be developed without any serious curtailment of the freedom of voluntary enlistment. Short of this, however, it ought to be easily possible to improve upon the present method of entry examination at the recruiting centres by a recognition of certain very simple but very important psychological facts and principles.

The broad problem of " choosing the recruit " consequently leads us to discuss :

(1) The type of examination to which all recruits should be submitted, the main purpose of which is to eliminate the unfit and so to maintain unimpaired efficiency.

(2) The further type of examination to which those who are provisionally accepted should be submitted, the main purpose of which is to recommend successful candidates to those particular army occupations for which they are best adapted.

I propose in this chapter to deal only with the first of these questions, and with this only in so far as it concerns the testing of the special senses.

The psychologist first comes into the field of the

general admission examination in relation to the testing of the special senses. Usually a candidate for the army is expected to reach a certain standard of capacity in vision and in hearing. In some cases he must be able to pass additional tests in colour discrimination and to display proficiency in other sensory processes. A very good case could be made out for the application to all recruits of certain simple tests of muscular control and co-ordination. I can say nothing here as to the exact details of any of the recognised methods of testing. They are the concern of the laboratory psychologist, both as regards their technique and as regards the normal standard of performance that may be demanded. Details are to be found in any modern text-book of psychology.[1] As a matter of fact, in spite of the great amount of work which has been done upon the special senses of man, there is still need for much research, whether in vision, in hearing, or in any other sensory process, in order that the type of test most valuable for military purposes should be determined. I propose here simply to take a single illustration and to show the main general points of importance that ought to be observed in arranging and applying tests of this kind.

It is usually supposed that tests of keenness of vision are particularly important in relation to the army. No doubt this is because the bulk of the men

[1] E.g. Myers, *Text-Book of Experimental Psychology*, Part I, and Myers and Bartlett, *Text-Book of Experimental Psychology*, Part II. Cambridge, 1925.

drafted into the fighting arms of military service may have to learn to shoot, and it seems on the face of it as if a fairly high standard of keenness of vision must be demanded unless shooting efficiency is to become dangerously low.

Although this is far less certain than may appear, everybody must agree that visual tests of some kind are important. Now the common tests of visual "acuity"—or, as it is often termed in general conversation, "keen eyesight"—are of two kinds. The first yield a measure of a man's capacity to recognise and distinguish shapes, forms, boundaries ; the second a measure of the accuracy of his discrimination of the light from the dark parts of an object. The commonest test of the first kind is the almost universally used "alphabet" test. With this a man's visual acuity is measured in terms of his capacity to identify and name individual letters of the alphabet which are presented to him under standard conditions as regards lighting, size and distance. Perhaps the most common test of the second kind is the "broken ring" test, in which a white or a black circle on a black or a white ground is broken at a certain point on its circumference. The circle is rotated by the experimenter, and the observer indicates the position at which he judges the break to occur. The position of the break may be reported with considerable accuracy although the observer may not be able to distinguish the exact dimensions and boundaries, either of the circle or of the missing part of it.

No doubt, for purposes of every-day visual observation, detection of the differences between shapes is extremely important, and so the common procedure, which employs the alphabet test, is well grounded. This is, for example, the kind of test which any man who is to be drafted into an observational unit should be required to pass. But the purpose of a general visual test as a part of a preliminary examination for the army is simply to rule out all men whose standard of vision is so low that they may be definitely dangerous when they are given fire-arms and can never make even moderately good "shots"; and for ordinary purposes of shooting, particularly such shooting as is possible for the mass of the rank and file in a modern war, it is doubtful whether a high degree of ability in the discrimination of forms is in any way essential.

The matter is one for experimental determination. We should take a group of first class "shots" and test their visual acuity by both methods. Then we should take a group of indifferent "shots," and a third group of definitely bad "shots" and test them in the same ways. There is already some evidence that no very high agreement holds between good visual acuity, as measured by the alphabet test, and shooting efficiency. Not only does it seem to be true that some who come out of the test well make bad "shots," but also—a matter of more importance—that a fair number who come badly out of the test nevertheless make good "shots," or fair "shots."

In the psychological laboratory at present there exist a number of "aiming" tests.[1] Actual experiment has shown that accuracy of aiming, particularly when the knack of the necessary muscular effort and co-ordination has been acquired, depends much less than might be expected upon visual factors.

Everybody knows that the efficient use of a rifle depends upon very many other conditions besides a clear view of the object aimed at. Much, for example, turns upon steadiness of muscular control, and even more upon the ability to make certain muscular contractions without at the same time making others. A man should, for instance, be able to contract one finger without at the same time contracting the muscles which control movements of the other fingers, of the arm, or of the shoulder. All good "shots" can do this; probably all mediocre "shots" can do it to some extent. The experimental psychologist, with his strong tendency to see problems in the concrete and his effort to find out directly the exact conditions of specific activities, must desire to see that both the initial tests and the methods of training should give sufficient attention to conditions which are other than visual. It might well be the case that a simple "positional" visual test, such as that of the broken ring, supplemented by some equally simple tests of muscular control and co-ordination, would be adequate.

A preliminary general examination must, as I have said, be mainly directed to the elimination of

----

[1] See, e.g. Myers and Bartlett, *op. cit.* 75.

the unfit. It is therefore extremely important, alike for efficiency and for fairness, that the tests imposed should be so fundamental that any man who fails at them is bound to fail at the work which he desires to pursue. For example, a deaf telephone operator would obviously be useless. But it is by no means so certain that a soldier with low visual efficiency as measured by the alphabet test is bound to fail as a "shot," or be dangerous when he has to use fire-arms.

Meanwhile, if the common alphabet test is retained, it requires much reformation. The ordinary alphabetical letters are by no means all equally visible. As distance from a letter increases, the visibility of different letters diminishes at different rates. At present letters of good and letters of poor visibility are commonly mixed up in a more or less haphazard way. Moreover mistakes in identification are not equally serious. To mistake *C* for *G*, for instance, is a trivial error. To mistake *C* for *B* may be significant. The visibility and correct grouping of letters have been accurately determined[1] in the psychological laboratory, and both the test-type cards and the methods of testing must in future be arranged with these results in view.

It would be possible to take all the other tests of special sense activities and submit them to the same sort of examination: tests of colour discrimination, of perception of movement, of judgment of

[1] See, e.g. Banister, 'Block Capital Letters in Tests of Acuity,' *Brit. Journ. of Ophthalmology*, Feb. 1927.

distance; tests of muscular control and co-ordination, and numerous others. They must not be taken over and used just as they have been arranged for purposes of general physiological and psychological research. They must be constructed, modified and applied with strict attention to army conditions and military needs. Every activity of the special senses is very complex. In real life now one set of conditions is pre-eminent, and now another. Practical tests must never lose sight of this fact.

It will be said that all this is merely "common sense." It is, however, the sort of common sense which it often seems to take a psychologist to appreciate at its full value. He appreciates it because it is his business to study the complex determination of concrete human activities, and to understand how this may vary with a variation in the practical problems which a given activity is called upon to solve.

Chapter II. THE GENERAL EXAMINATION

THE general entrance examination to the army at present consists commonly of a medical examination and a few tests of visual and other special sense activities. It is, however, often urged that some investigation of intelligence should be added.

When the American nation decided to enter the late European War they were faced with a huge practical problem very different from that of any other belligerent people. They had to build up an army out of extremely heterogeneous elements drawn from nearly all the more or less civilised nations on the face of the earth, and to deal with a very large number of most illiterate persons. All this had to be done hurriedly. In peace-time a man can be moved about from unit to unit, or from occupation to occupation, until at last something is found that he can do fairly well, in a social environment to which he can adapt himself successfully. Even in peace-time this involves a great waste of time, money and effort; in war-periods it may be far more immediately dangerous. It is easy to argue that the work of the private soldier does not demand a high degree of intelligence, but there is in practice a minimum of intelligence below which it is dangerous to fall. Moreover the more specialised is the type of task which a man is asked to perform, the more pressing, as a rule, are the demands upon his intelligence. There is some evidence also that a direct relation exists between intellectual rank and capacity for responsibility, so that whenever officers and N.C.O's. have to be made in a hurry, any simple and fairly reliable method of assessing intelligence may have immediate practical importance.

A Psychology Division was formed as a branch of the Medical Section of the American War Department. Special officers were trained in the principles and technique of mental tests, and by November 1918 over a million and a half recruits had been tested in this way.

There were three aims underlying the experiment: (1) to eliminate all men whose grade of intelligence was so low that they were bound to be a burden and a danger to the service; (2) to find out and use in special ways all men whose superior intelligence seemed to fit them for speedy advancement; (3) to select men who had peculiar capabilities especially suited to certain particular military duties. The movement was so organised that an examining staff at a camp could test, on an average, 2000 men every day and have their ranking of the candidates ready to report within another twenty-four hours. It is claimed that this ranking rendered possible an extremely rapid and satisfactory sorting of men in the Depôt Brigades, all commissioned and non-com-

missioned officers being selected from among the
men who reached certain grades of intelligence as
determined by the tests; and all those who fell
below a certain standard being rejected as incapable
and unsafe.[1]

It was, then, on the basis of the mental as sup-
plemental to the medical test that men were taken
into the American army, and on the same basis
largely that they were graded, once they had been
accepted.

Obviously, in order to decide anything about the
claims of the mental test movement in relation to
the organisation of an army, we must know what
ideas underlie the notion of an intelligence-test, what
mental processes are in general assessed in this way,
and how far the methods employed should be looked
upon solely as a war-time expedient useful mainly
because they economise time.

Probably everybody, at some time or another, has
distinguished *attainments* from *intelligence*. We say of
a certain person: "He is a clever man, but he does
not know very much"; of another: "He is really
stupid, but by hard work he has acquired a lot of
knowledge." Attainments are mainly, though not
entirely, a matter of special environment, and particularly of social tradition. Intelligence we take to
mean not what a man has learned, but his capacity
to learn. Most ordinary examinations try to discover
how far a person has profited from a certain course
of training. The intelligence-test attempts to find

[1] See *Army Mental Tests*, Washington, D.C., U.S.A., 1918.

out how a person may be expected to profit from *any* course of training.

Undoubtedly no test of intelligence can be devised which does not to some extent rest upon knowledge that has been acquired. We have to assume a knowledge of the meanings of common words; or, if we are dealing with different language groups or with very illiterate people, a knowledge of the meaning of common pictorial forms and representations. But the structure of modern society is such that everybody has a fair chance to learn these rudiments of knowledge, and if he has not done so we may safely conclude that he so far lacks the common human motives as to be practically useless in any group of normal persons, or that he is definitely deficient in intellect.

There is a further point. The ordinary examination, meant to test one man's intelligence, really tests the intelligence of two : that of the candidate and that of the examiner. Upon the examiner's intelligence depends the validity of the marks which he gives to a candidate's performance. Thus the candidate's intelligence-rank depends, not directly or solely upon his performance, but upon the examiner's opinion of his performance, and, as everybody knows, clashing opinions are common.

The intelligence-test movement devises sets of questions to which perfectly definite answers are demanded. It gives the questions to large numbers of individuals of the type with which it proposes to deal. Comparison of the results shows what standard of correct answers can be taken to represent the normal within such a group, and what may be regarded as exceptional in either direction from the normal. In theory it makes no difference who sets or marks the questions or answers. In practice the matter is less simple than this, and special training is needed in the conduct of a mental test examination. The marking is, however, standardised, and the caprice of the examiner is wholly eliminated.

The two important ideas underlying the use of intelligence-tests are thus: (1) to distinguish capacity to learn from acquirements of knowledge, and to test the former: (2) to eliminate liability to error through the personal idiosyncrasies of the examiner.

Often it is said that there is a third underlying notion, namely, that what is called intelligence is a *general* factor, so that all mental skill of whatsoever kind and in whatsoever direction is the expression, at least in part, of the same basic mental activity. Whether this is the case, however, is still a matter of controversy. In practice it does not make much difference whether intelligence is the single activity of one underlying character, or whether it is a collection, or group, of different activities.

In order to see what mental processes are involved in their solution, we must have a few characteristic instances of the tests before us. The number of tests which have been proposed and used is legion, but the principles of their construction are comparatively few, and of these few those which have been shown to have a definite significance in practice are still fewer. I shall select and discuss one or two tests, so that we may be able to form some notion of what, in this connexion, is meant by "intelligence."

It must be fully understood that the *only* justification of the tests which I am about to illustrate is their usefulness in practice. Their value is now fully established in many different directions, so that the only valid destructive criticism of them must be based upon actual experience. At first sight they are apt, particularly when only a small selection of examples can be given, to appear very much of the nature of "trick work." They have undoubtedly often to be freely adapted for the precise purpose in hand. In particular, they may need to be suited to illiterate or semi-illiterate candidates. But these adaptations are not difficult to make and in many directions have been made already.

Again, no psychologist whose knowledge of human nature has not been entirely swept aside by his enthusiasm for his science would want to argue that they form in themselves an entirely sufficient system of tests. The temperamental factor, as I shall again and again point out, is extremely important, and the intelligence-test by itself gives but little insight into this. The practice, often adopted, of getting into closer touch with men during periods of "standing at ease," asking them questions about their homes, their interests, their county, their work and their sports is to be most warmly encouraged. Yet, making due allowance for the value of all this, there still remains plenty of room for the application of soundly devised tests of intelligence in a period as near as possible to the time at which a man enters the army.

A test which finds a place in nearly every collection that has been proposed is the "analogies" test. The candidate is given a form upon which a number of rows of words are printed. First he is told to read the instructions which run: "In each of the horizontal lines below, the first two names are related to each other in some way. See what the relation is between the first two names, and underline the word in SMALL CAPITALS that is related in the same manner to the third name. Begin at Number 1, and work through as much as you can before 'time' is called. For example:

White is to Black as Day is to: SUN, WINTER, NIGHT, STAR.

(Black is the opposite to White, and hence Night, which is the opposite to Day, is underlined.)

Window is to House as Soldier is to: SAILOR, MAN, FIGHTER, ARMY.

(Window is part of a House, and hence Army, of of which a Soldier is part, is underlined.)

1. Pen is to Writing as Tongue is to: EATING, TALKING, MOUTH, SCRIPT.

2. Violet is to Flower as Mule is to: ANIMAL, OBSTINACY, HORSE, TRANSPORT.

3. Evil is to Wickedness as Happiness is to: MISERY, POVERTY, JOY, WEALTH."

The test then goes on to give about twenty examples of analogies arranged in this way.

Answering a test of this kind is usually said to depend upon a candidate's ability to "appreciate relations." The process is far from a simple one, however, and seeing that there are excellent reasons for holding that it enters pre-eminently into all intelligent behaviour, and seeing also that it is, to the best of my knowledge, demanded by all intelligence-tests which have proved of real use, we must discuss it more thoroughly.

A man walking along a crowded pathway and at the same time thinking deeply makes constant adjustments of direction, of speed, of the swing of his arms and the balance of his body in order to avoid collision with other people. These adjustments mean that he is reacting in some way to the positions of other folk in relation to those of himself. But he is aware of only a few of his adjustments, if of any. He could give no account of them afterwards, and he does not formulate the relations involved at the time in order to act upon them. Similarly a man riding a motor-bicycle at high speed round a corner, or round a bend of a track, adjusts his position to that of the machine, and both to the tilt and direction of the road, so as to maintain an undisturbed balance. He does this without formulation, and very likely if he were asked to state in general terms what exactly he would do in that kind of emergency, he would be at a loss to say. Behaviour of this type may reach a high degree of complexity. In an International Rugby football match played a few years ago between England

and Wales one of the Welsh players, near the end
of the game, suffered a slight concussion. He was
able to continue playing, and actually initiated and
carried on a concerted movement which ended in his
scoring a spectacular "try." Nevertheless he could
give no account of anything that had happened after
his concussion. In all these instances the adjustments made depend upon a capacity to react to
relative positions, speed, distances, directions,
and so on, of the different elements in a complex
situation. But these relations are reacted to only in
so far as they are parts of that particular concrete
situation which is immediately present. They are not
formulated or described in general terms applicable
to *any* situation in which the same sort of central
problem may occur.

Now the outstanding fact about that appreciation of relations which is the main feature of many
intelligence-tests is that the relations which are dealt
with must be formulated. An instance of a relation
between words, or pictures, or digits is provided and
the candidate is asked to pick out another instance
of the same relation, the terms now being different
ones. Sometimes this is done in an automatic,
habitual manner. For example, when a person reads:

White is to Black as Day is to:

he commonly runs on in his mind to "Night" in
as completely unthinking a way as he alters the
swing of his arm, or the direction of his bodily
movement, so as to avoid hitting an approaching
foot-passenger in a crowded pathway. He is, in fact,

merely unrolling a simple word habit. But in many cases, in order that he should select the right fourth word, or picture, or digit, he must formulate the relation in some way, realising—though he may not actually use words: "Here is a relation of opposition, or of part to whole, or of agent and action," and so on.

This formulation is exactly what the man who is commonly called intelligent constantly carries out in daily life. He copes with a continually changing environment by using methods of behaviour which he has learned in a setting different from the one immediately facing him. He has to be able to see that though the details dealt with may be new, the principles involved are old. Having, for example, learned to drive, control, and repair one type of motor-car, he rapidly adapts himself to a different one. Whenever we state that a man works with understanding or insight, we mean that he can, in some concrete situation, so grasp the connexions of the details with which he must deal that, even when some of the details are changed, he can still make the suitable response. At least that is an important part of what we mean. The fact that a well-designed analogies-test demands the exercise of this capacity is what gives it its indisputable value as a means of assessing intelligence.

Another test which gives very good results depends upon ability to grasp the law underlying the construction of a series of numbers, of pictorial forms, or of other material employed for special purposes. For example, a section of such a test runs:

"Give the number that comes next in each of the following lines:

1	3	9	27	81	243	(	).
96	48	24	12	6	3	(	).
9	8	7	6	7	8	(	).[1]"

Here a candidate is required to discover the relation between one term and another, to recognise several instances of the same relation, to realise in some way the law governing the continuation of the series, and on the basis of this himself to provide a new term. This is different from the type of analogies-test just illustrated, in that instead of merely *recognising* an instance of a relation, the candidate must *construct* a new instance of a given relation.

A somewhat different form of the same test requires the candidate to detect and eliminate some fact or detail which ought not to be in the series within which it is presented. For example: "Cross out the 'extra' word in each of the following lines:

charity, kindness, benevolence, revenge, love.

square, circular, oblong, hexagonal, triangular.

hair, feathers, wool, glass, fur."

Or again: "Cross out the extra numbers in each of the following lines:

26	3	7	31	13	17.
81	27	11	1	9	3.
7	28	21	35	14	27.[2]"

[1] See Godfrey Thomson, 'The Northumberland Mental Tests,' *Brit. Journ. of Psychol.* XII, 201 ff. These tests may be obtained from Messrs Harrap and Co., Ltd.

[2] Each of the last two illustrations is taken from Thomson, *op. cit.*

As before, tests of this type demand in most cases the appreciation of the law of a series. It is, however, probably an easier task to eliminate an irrelevant detail than to produce a relevant one.

There are a great many other tests which might well be considered. But I have given sufficient illustrations to show some of their most important guiding principles. In details the tests differ widely, but the most successful of them all tend to bring in the same demands for *analysis* of a more or less complex situation, *appreciation of the way in which the elements of that situation are built together*, and the *recognition* of the same relations in new situations, the *production* of a new situation involving the same relations, or the *elimination* of some irrelevant detail. These may be said to be the outstanding characteristics of intelligence according to the psychologists who have framed and who employ mental tests.

We have now to consider whether mental tests, as part of a general entrance examination, should be regarded merely as a war-time expedient, useful only or mainly when an army has to be organised in a hurry. The advantages and drawbacks of the use of intelligence-tests have been the subject of a great amount of research for several years past, and I shall first state, without discussion, certain facts which may be regarded as established.

1. Intelligence-tests can certainly be devised, applied rapidly and marked definitely, with a considerable saving of time as compared with the more ordinary written examination.

2. Such tests do undoubtedly discover those persons whose intellectual capacity is so low that they are very unlikely to profit by any course of training demanding even a small degree of intelligence. Conversely the tests indicate also persons of superior intellectual equipment.

3. For children and academic ability certainly, for adults and their general capacity less certainly, the results of the application of tests agree remarkably well with those of the more time-consuming methods of assessing intelligence.

4. The fact that tests applied to a *group* of candidates must in general be speed tests does not invalidate their results.

5. Practice, or coaching, in tests of the kind proposed makes very little, if any, difference to the relative ranking of candidates as judged by the test results.

Thus, in general, the tests can certainly be used to eliminate the intellectually unfit. Can they be equally relied upon to select the intellectually fit? Here we are on less safe ground. Statistically it is clear that men who come well out of a suitably arranged intelligence-test examination will also probably succeed in that combination of intelligence, practical skill and temperamental balance which army life demands. But there is room for much error so far as individuals are concerned.

For example, a large number of Air Force apprentices were recently examined by certain well-known "reasoning" tests and in other ways. The

mechanic apprentice in the Air Force has to pass
both a written and a practical examination at the
end of his probationary period and his academic
and trade status are determined by these. In general
the results of the tests and those of the examinations agreed fairly well, but there were some
marked discrepancies. The top man according to
the tests ranked low according to the examinations.
This undoubtedly was partly due to the fact that the
examination places much emphasis upon mechanical
skill, the tests none. Mechanical skill and abstract
intellectual capacity probably have little in common.
But by far the most important point was that this
man was temperamentally ill-suited to his environment. He considered the branch of the Air Force
in which he was engaged not good enough for him,
his companions as belonging to a different level
socially and intellectually, and himself as too big a
man to be kept at small, unnoticed and trivial tasks.
He possessed in fact high intellectual capacity, but
also a temperamental endowment which, in the
position in which he had to live, prevented that
capacity from finding expression.

For practical purposes temperament is a more
important factor in success than intelligence, as the
latter is understood in the mental test movement.
Slight variations in temperament may make a bigger
difference to a man's practical value in any social
organisation such as an army than large variations
in intellectual processes. No doubt much can be
done by psychological experiment to discover a

man's real temperamental qualities; no doubt a psychologically skilled or a psychologically trained observer can detect such qualities speedily and with reasonable accuracy. But the satisfactory direct temperament-test has yet to be devised, and very likely never will be found.

On the whole, then, by intelligence-tests a man may be safely ruled out, but by intelligence-tests alone a man cannot safely be ruled in.

Is it worth doing the former? This is a purely practical question, and there are hardly sufficient data available for a definite answer. In my opinion, however, the expenditure of time, money and effort, and the severe demands upon temper and general control which the presence of exceedingly stupid men in an army unit are apt to entail are not genuinely worth the slight numerical advantage which their retention may give.

I have discussed this problem as if it were the direct concern of the army. But it really raises some very broad and fundamental issues. It ought to be realised more fully than it sometimes appears to be that the community is as much the servant of its fighting forces as its fighting forces are the servants of the community. Intellectual capacity and temperamental endowment are relatively stable parts of a man's life. In all probability school records of these remain valid for later life in the great majority of cases. The school is the proper place for intelligence-tests and for systematic observations of temperament. In future, when a man presents himself for entry to any important social group in his country, the records of his intelligence-rating and of his temperamental make-up ought to be as readily available as his ordinary health records. If these were made seriously at the proper time, the problems of building and training an efficient army would be considerably simplified.

Finally, it is of the very greatest importance that, in the case of the officer at least, a general admission examination to the army should include some examination of the candidate's liability to nervous and mental disorder under conditions of war strain. The factors that are of importance in this respect can, however, be much more clearly shown after a discussion of some of the common mental troubles of warfare. Accordingly I shall postpone my treatment of this matter for the present.

Chapter III. CHOOSING THE RECRUIT

TESTS OF SPECIAL ABILITIES

A GENERAL examination shows whether or not a man is fit for army service, but it does not show for what kind of service in the army he is fit. The problem of sorting and classifying candidates and assigning or recommending them to the special duties for which they are best fitted is, however, one of continually increasing importance. About six hundred different instruction courses are now in progress (1926) in the British Army. Each makes its own special demands on those who take part in it, and each can help to build up an efficient branch of the service only in so far as it has the right type of man to deal with. A modern army is, in fact, both for complexity and for specialised activity comparable with modern industrial organisation. In both it is common to meet individuals who are set to work for which their physical and mental aptitudes thoroughly unfit them. Such individuals inevitably waste time, money, temper, and are an obstacle to the maintenance of discipline and the development of *morale*. Many of the resulting difficulties could perfectly easily be overcome by the use of psychological tests for special abilities.

When we turn from a general admission examination to the further testing of those who have already passed the first stage, the main purpose of our tests changes at once. We can no longer be satisfied with eliminating the unfit, but must definitely decide what the fit are to be asked to do. It might seem as if there is little need of special tests for this purpose. Why not rely upon a candidate's interests or preferences?

This question has many times been investigated during recent years, and it can be shown:

(*a*) That a large number of persons have no well-marked preferences or interests, but nevertheless are by no means equally good in all kinds of skilled tasks;

(*b*) That interests are highly fluctuating in early years and even up to a fairly late period of life;

(*c*) That ability does not necessarily follow interest, and that the proportion of cases in which it does is smaller than is popularly believed.[1]

Interest therefore, save in very well-marked cases, if even then, cannot by itself be taken as a safe guide to ability.

We are driven back upon two alternatives. We may either follow the usual practice and assign a man to any task for which there is an obvious vacancy, trusting more or less to luck that he will settle down and become reasonably efficient in

[1] See especially: Douglas Fryer, 'Intelligence and Interest in Vocational Adjustment,' *Pedagogical Seminary*, xxx, 1923, 127–51, and 'The Significance of Interest for Vocational Prognosis,' *Mental Hygiene*, vii, 1924, 466–505.

time; or we may try to find out by special tests whether or not he is likely to perform a given task well. If the second method can be proved successful, it must obviously be far more economical in every way than the first, and it is also likely to produce a higher standard of efficiency. Fortunately it has been repeatedly proved by experiment that the method of vocational tests is both practicable and successful.

I propose first to describe briefly an actual experiment in vocational selection, and second to indicate the main types of vocational tests and their underlying principles.

Among the devices which were used to detect submarines during the late war were a number which depended essentially upon an operator's ability to hear, identify and localise the sound made by the vessels in travelling through the water. When the hydrophone service, which was concerned with the use of these devices, was first organised, volunteers were asked for, and all those who were generally fit, in a medical sense, and for whom vacancies could be found, were accepted. The same thing then happened that has often occurred in other instances, both in the Navy and in the Army. "Trained" men not infrequently proved relatively useless in practice and had to give way to others who had been "trained" little or not at all. It then seemed worth while to try to see if suitable tests could be devised, as a result of the application of which it could be foretold whether a man would be likely to become efficient under training or not. It was hoped that the tests would show not only whether a man was fit for hydrophone service, but also to what type of instrument he should be sent, for different devices required different capacities. Preliminary experiments looked promising, and ultimately all volunteers for the hydrophone service were required to pass a number of special tests. These I will very briefly describe.

(1) A general medical examination in reference to hearing.

Not a few men who possessed no obvious physical defects in their mechanism of hearing nevertheless could not carry out satisfactorily certain simple tasks of listening. This gives us a special case of the general truth that there is no immediate conclusion that structural fitness involves functional fitness.

2. A group test of auditory acuity, designed solely for the purpose of eliminating all candidates whose standard of hearing fell below a certain level.[1]

3. An examination based on simple tests of intelligence of the kind already referred to, and also used solely for the purpose of eliminating the unfit.

4. Two simple special tests bearing directly upon the work required of a hydrophone operator:

(*a*) a test in accuracy of rapid reading from a scale;

(*b*) a test of ability to understand the construction of simple mechanical and electrical apparatus from diagrams.

[1] See Myers and Bartlett, *op. cit.* 48–51.

5. A series of special tests giving measures of:

(*a*) capacity to recognise sounds;

(*b*) capacity to recognise rhythm of sounds;

(*c*) capacity to recognise pitch of sounds;

(*d*) capacity to recognise differences in intensity of sounds;

(*e*) capacity to recognise position and change of position of sounds.

On the basis of their test performances men were selected and allocated to particular types of work. The administration of the tests took only a relatively short time. The experiment undoubtedly succeeded in detecting the men who could be trained speedily to a high degree of efficiency and who in practice proved keen, interested and contented. It should be admitted that the tests did not have a very long period of trial before the end of the war came, but it is not too much to say that the general standard of capacity in the hydrophone service was considerably increased by the use of these methods. In much the same way tests for selection or fitness have been widely used in connection with various branches of the Air Service, of artillery work, and of many other departments of military organisation where special skill is called for. In the great majority of cases, where the tests have been devised and administered under adequate psychological supervision, they have proved their practical usefulness.

It is of interest to consider briefly some of the principles underlying the construction of tests used for the detection of special abilities. The methods adopted lead, as is now generally recognised, to four main types of test. "We may," says Professor Cyril Burt, "term them respectively the methods of 'sample' tests; 'analogous' tests; 'empirical' tests, and 'analytic' tests. In the sample tests the operation measured is a typical example of the work actually to be done. In the analogous test the operation to be measured is not identical with the work to be done but is merely similar to it psychologically. In the empirical test the operation measured is chosen, not for its apparent identity with or similarity to the work to be carried out, but simply because in actual practice it has proved an effective test, although the reasons for its effectiveness are perhaps neither obvious nor clear. In the analytic test an endeavour is made to resolve the work into its elementary psychological constituents."[1]

The analytic method is clearly illustrated in the tests for hydrophone operators which have already been mentioned. Each element in a complex response—appreciation of pitch, intensity, rhythm and locality of sounds, together with certain more purely mental capacities—was separately tested. There is one great difficulty attending the use of such a method. A man may possess each of the abilities required for a complicated task and yet not be able to bring them into play in a harmonious and efficient manner when the task as a whole has to be performed.

[1] *Lectures on Industrial Administration*, Ed. B. Muscio, London, 1920, 88.

It is almost impossible to lay down rules which will show when an analytic method can be used and when it may give misleading results. Probably, however, when a man is to be asked to carry out reactions in a fixed serial order, this method of testing is adequate and valuable. This is notably the case in numerous relatively mechanical industrial tasks, and also in many army occupations where skill in detail has to be united with a fairly fixed order of succession in work. When the different elements of a complex task have constantly to change places with one another, to be rearranged so as to suit the immediate circumstances of the moment; when they possess no fixed order and no one always predominating unit, the analytical method used by itself is apt to be unsatisfactory. The psychological reason for this is that a straightforward *seria,* arrangement of reactions is the most natural and the simplest to acquire, so that a man who possesses the necessary abilities can very easily acquire the capacity to arrange and control them in serial fashion. But constant rearrangement in response to the exigencies of the moment is a more difficult matter altogether and demands much more than the mere possession of the abilities to be expressed. No doubt this is why we often find, for example, that a man who has all the abilities required for first-rate success at games nevertheless may completely fail on the actual field of play. For the skilled activities of a game can hardly ever be unrolled like a habit; they must take any order to meet the needs of the moment.

An empirical test is simply one which has been proved by repeated experience to be satisfactory, although nobody can say very clearly why it should be so. The method underlying the discovery and employment of empirical tests has been well described by H. L. Hollingworth. He is dealing with occupational tests for the discovery of special industrial abilities:

A group of workers whose relative abilities in the work in question are already fairly well known and capable of expression in quantitative, or at least in relative terms, is chosen. To these individuals, good, average and poor, are given as many tests as the patience of the worker, the zeal of the experimenter, or the interest of the employer makes possible. Ability in each test is then compared with ability in the work. Certain tests may in this way be found which serve as indices of occupational capacity—good workers perform these tests well, poor workers do them poorly. Of thirty or forty tests thus tried out, perhaps only four or five will seem to possess this diagnostic significance, and only these four or five are retained as tests for the type of ability in question.[1]

In all this there is no attempt to analyse either the work or the test, or to find out the psychological reasons why success in the latter correlates well with success in the former. There is, for example, no very obvious connexion between controlling an aeroplane and reading with understanding a complicated argument under conditions of diminished oxygen pressure. Yet it is fairly constantly found

[1] Hollingworth and Poffenberger, *Applied Psychology*, New York, 1918, 196–7.

that a man who can do the second can also, assuming satisfactory technical knowledge of course, successfully do the first. An empirical test, in fact, is simply one which has proved its worth in actual experience, although the reasons for its value have not been worked out either before or after its application. However, as time goes on, fewer and fewer vocational tests are of this somewhat "hit or miss" order.

"Analogous" tests, which have been used by psychologists very widely and with great success, have been clearly described by Professor Cyril Burt.

Such tests [he says] endeavour to reproduce on a small scale a situation similar to that involved in the real life of the candidate. The similarity, however, must be internal or subjective rather than external and superficial. The test situation resembles the actual situation in the sense that the former seems likely to call forth the same mental processes as are required by the latter. Outward similarity is valueless. In naval courts, where ship collisions are demonstrated by means of miniature models, the most experienced navigator is apt to become confused; the perceptions, the interests, the decisions aroused by the toy ships sliding on a piece of glass are not those excited by real vessels at sea. It is the inner attitude of mind, and not the external shape and colour of the objects, that the tests must transplant into the laboratory.[1]

The assumption underlying all such tests is that like tests demand like capacities. The success of the tests in practice has justified this assumption, provided that sufficient care is taken to see that the

[1] *Op. cit.* 88–9.

tasks are really like. For example, reaction-time tests have been of considerable service in the examination of aviators. "Reaction-time" is the name given to the period which elapses between the appearance of a stimulus and the response which a man makes to that stimulus. The tests are of three main types and are often known as "Simple Reaction tests," "Discrimination Reaction tests," and "Choice Reaction tests." In the first a "single" stimulus has always to be followed by some simple prescribed response. A man is asked, for instance, to lift his finger from a morse key as soon as he hears a certain sound or sees the flash of a light. In the second there are a number of different stimuli, and response is not to be made until the precise stimulus given has been recognised. Thus there may be sounds differing in pitch, or lights differing in colour, or both. They all have to be followed by the same simple response, but that response must not be made until the precise sound or colour presented has been discriminated. In the third form there are a variety of stimuli which may be given in haphazard order, and for each one the correct response is different from the response required to any of the others. Obviously a Choice Reaction test can be arranged so as to call for much the same capacities as are required for the efficient and speedy control of various more or less complex forms of mechanism where delicate adjustments have to be made very quickly to constantly varying stimuli. It is in this form that the test has proved of service in the examination of airmen. Mere speed of reaction is not, however, the only, or the most important matter. More weight must be laid upon the *distribution* of reactions, for a man who shows unusual speed, but sudden lapses, may be far more dangerous than the man who, though less speedy, is extremely consistent.

Finally "sample" tests are the plan, already adopted by many employers or trainers, of a probationary period. It is assumed that if a man can carry out a short task with success he will probably successfully tackle a long job of the same kind. In a very large number of cases this by no means holds good. All tests of this type demand careful psychological control. The diagnostic significance of short spells of work must be determined separately for each type of task. The "sample" test is peculiarly liable to be disturbed by the fact that many men set to a brief spell of work, unconsciously exert themselves to produce results which they fail to maintain, while other men suffer unduly from the fact that they are slow to "warm up" to a job. An examiner who uses this kind of test will fail completely unless all the time he keeps a careful eye on the temperamental make-up of his subjects.

To some extent this final observation applies to all of the tests of vocational aptitude. They provide work for the *psychologist*, and may be dangerous in the hands of the untrained examiner. They must be devised, applied, and their results evaluated with psychological considerations constantly before the mind. As Dr C. S. Myers has often pointed out,[1] it is not enough to discover *what* a man can do ; his *way of doing it* may be of even greater importance. Because it is very easy to make up amusing tests, to apply them, and then to present an imposing array of statistical results, there is no field in which psychological quackery is more rampant. There is also, in all probability, no field of practice in which genuine psychological insight can win more splendid success. Vocational tests, committed to the care of the untrained enthusiast, as they have often been, are very frequently a mere waste of time, effort and money. But if they are devised, applied and interpreted with true psychological knowledge, the case is different. They may then, without doubt, be of great service in building up an efficient and, what is much the same and equally important, a contented group.

There is another movement in contemporary psychology which is closely allied to that of vocational tests, and which has equal applicability to many problems of army organisation. A careful study of the incidence of industrial accidents has shown that there exists an "accident prone" class of persons.[2] Given equal objective risks, an individual who belongs to this class will tend to have more accidents than, according to pure chance, he ought to have. This is probably true of major accidents involving loss of life or of limb, and it is certainly true of

[1] See, e.g. *Industrial Psychology in Great Britain*, London, 1925.
[2] See especially : 'A Contribution to the Study of the Human Factor in the Causation of Accidents,' by E. M. Newbold, *Report of the Industrial Fatigue Research Board*, No. 34.

minor accidents which, involving loss of time, temper, personal prestige, self-confidence and the like, are not less troublesome, though they may be less spectacular than a great "smash up." The question therefore arises whether it is possible by means of special tests to diagnose a man's liability to accident. Apparently it is going to be perfectly possible to do this. There is no space here to describe the tests which have already been tried.[1] They have met with encouraging success. They are for the most part somewhat complicated tests involving the co-ordination of a number of different bodily activities. Here also the difficult questions of temperamental determination and control are to the front. It is probably not too much to say that in a few years from now the psychologist will be able to assess with considerable accuracy a man's accident risk for a given class of work. The matter will obviously not stop short at this point, for once such a risk is known, the next thing is to discover what steps can be taken to minimise it and to prevent its becoming a serious menace. Both diagnosis and prevention in the matter of accident liability are matters of vital concern to an army. They are both, in part, fundamentally psychological problems.

[1] See: 'A Psychological Study of Individual Differences in Accident Rates,' by Eric Farmer and E. G. Chambers, *Industrial Fatigue Research Board Report*, No. 38, London, 1926.

Chapter IV. TRAINING BODILY SKILL

THE recruit having been accepted and sent to that particular branch of the Service for which his aptitudes best fit him, the next question that arises concerns the ways in which he should be trained. Everybody agrees that the training must not be merely haphazard, and, as can of course be seen by a glance at any one of the many manuals of Army Training, it has already, in the British Army, been very highly organised in many directions. But in order to justify any of the special features of a course of training some kind of psychological reason must be found. For example, why has it been customary, in teaching infantry drill, to adopt the plan of breaking up a set of more or less complex movements into their constituent elements and then of taking each part by itself? The reason must be that in human learning processes a complicated pattern of movement can in general be most quickly acquired and be longest remembered by this way of taking it piecemeal. Both of these are psychological statements, and have to do with how the human mind as well as with how the human body works. Whether we are trying to train a man's body to perform skilled movements, or to teach the man himself how to endure pain and hardship and to control his general behaviour by ideals of loyalty, patriotism and good comradeship, the ultimate questions are always psychological questions.

For the present I shall be concerned solely with problems that arise in the teaching of skilled movement; I shall leave for later consideration the equally important questions of training a man to control his cruder instincts and emotions, by the ideals upon which a well-regulated army is based. The military importance of how best to teach skilled bodily movement is too obvious to need comment.

From the point of view of the onlooker, animal activity finds its most obvious expression in muscular contraction. Generally some stimulus, or a pattern of stimuli, belonging to the external world affects the bodily organism. As a result, impulses are conveyed along a complicated system of nerves by way of the spinal cord to the brain. Thereupon further impulses are set up in different nerve fibres, and these impulses pass out to a certain set of muscles which contract or relax, and an obvious bodily movement is the result. Once more, the movement of the muscles itself initiates impulses of the "sensory" type, and these carry to the brain a message which we are normally able to interpret to the effect that a movement has taken place. The interpretation of these final sensory impressions, which come from the bodily movements themselves, is, in common language, known as "the muscular sense." The bodily movement need not, of course, begin with an actually and immediately presented external stimulus. It may be set up as a result of a man's recollection and representation in mental imagery of some past event, or by a wish, or in other ways initiated within the organism itself ; but we need not be concerned with these at present.

Normally we are aware not only that a limb has moved, but also of the direction of the movement, and the relation of the part moved to other parts of the body. This is partly due to sensations whose origin is in the joints, and partly due to the fact that the sensitive tendons or sinews which attach the muscles to the bones also contribute towards the total effect which is produced when any limb changes its position.

Moreover, muscles fall broadly into antagonistic groups. There is, for instance, one group controlling flexion, another controlling extension, of the forearm. If one set is contracted, the other set must be relaxed. Should both at once be stimulated for contraction the result may be no movement, or a hesitating and faulty movement. Any cleanly executed set of bodily movements involves the simultaneous contraction and relaxation of a large number of muscles, and the function of bringing varied muscular activities into co-ordination is a matter mainly of the central nervous system. Thus in fatigue, as we shall see, the capacity to co-ordinate movements tends to be greatly disturbed. A given movement tends to pass too readily or immediately into its opposite, and the result is an increasing "feeling" of effort and a poorer and poorer performance.

It is an interesting fact that the vitally important sensory impulses which are set up by changes in muscles, joints and tendons commonly operate without our knowing anything whatever about them. The ordinary man, unless he happens to become specially interested in what bodily movements actually "feel like," never does know anything about them. That they are of the utmost importance to our bodily efficiency and well-being is clear from the unfortunate effects which follow their loss by disease or injury. But they are like a secret service which may constantly bring the most important information into a country although practically nobody in the country knows who they are, or even that they are there at all.

Probably for most of us the period in which we are genuinely interested in muscle-joint-tendon sensations comes early in life and is soon outgrown. The young child who has just learned to walk often seems to be persistently experimenting with his limbs, stretching them out, putting them into odd positions and trying new movements. He seems to find a genuine sensory pleasure in these experiments. But with a swiftly awakening interest in the external world this phase rapidly passes. Its passage is doubtless greatly facilitated by the use of language, which, in the forms that are current in any developed human group, is constructed mainly about adult interests. Thus it is not in the least surprising either that those few people who are acutely aware of their muscle sensations find the utmost difficulty in describing them, or that such people very often seem to have a somewhat childish and undeveloped outlook, as if they are still living partly in a phase of life which properly belongs to our earlier years.

Whatever may be the explanation, it is certain that the actual experience of a movement is extremely hard to describe, and that in this respect the muscle sense and that of vision are especially sharply contrasted. This has been forcibly pointed out by Professor T. H. Pear in his attractive book called *Skill in Work and Play*.[1]

"Let us imagine [he says] a lawn tennis player trying to describe the game to an intelligent foreigner who has never seen it. As the player speaks, before him, either actually or in his mind's eye, will be the green rectangular court, the white straight lines, the brown net with its white tape, the rackets and the players. To depict them successfully in words is easy, if only the player has a reasonably rich vocabulary, and the foreigner understands it. The outstanding features of strokes in the game can be expressed in visual terms, since most accounts of games lay stress upon or are exclusively devoted to their spectacular aspect.

But now let us suppose the foreigner to ask for an account of the game as the player feels it *from inside*; urges him to describe the sensations in his limbs when he changes his grip, steps into position for a back-hand drive, throws the weight of his body behind a smash, or makes a chop stroke. At once language is found to be less fluent, distinctions between words less subtle and clear-cut, the words themselves harder to find. As a result, our player, desperate after unsuccessful snatchings at a few solid words in the bog in which he is floundering, invites the politely persistent foreigner to watch him do the things.[2]

[1] London, 1924.   [2] *Op. cit.* 18-9.

Everybody recognises the truth of this as soon as it has been pointed out. It is a matter of great interest to turn the pages of the series of booklets known as the "New Blue Series,"[1] in which Cambridge Blues have attempted, generally with illuminating clarity, to show the way in which the game or sport in which they won fame should be practised. Anybody who is interested in teaching skill in bodily movement should study some or all of these. In every single case, from games such as cricket and Rugby football, to sports such as boxing, swimming and fencing, the descriptions are far more of movements as they can be seen than of movement as it can be felt.

Whether the difficulty of describing bodily skill in terms of what it feels like from inside is one that can be overcome with effort and practice is not yet clear. I think myself that the trouble is more deep seated, and that in all probability muscular sensations can perform their important functions smoothly only so long as we are not much aware of them or of their character. But in any case these considerations show that in teaching skill in movement very little can be done *easily* in terms of direct description of the bodily sensations which may arise when the skill is efficiently exercised.

Various more or less unsatisfactory attempts have been made to classify different types of skilled movement. Practically all teaching of bodily skill in the Army concerns the acquisition of complex move-

[1] Cambridge, 1922-3, Fabb and Tyler.

ments or series of movements the different items of which are already pretty well known, though they may now have to be combined in unfamiliar ways. This is the case, for example, with nearly all forms of drill. Sometimes, perhaps, genuinely new forms of bodily reaction may be demanded, as, for example, in some of the finger and arm movements of rifle-shooting. But here also the new movement is invariably a complex one, and can be resolved into elements which are familiar or at least relatively simple.

In practice these complex movements are nearly always analysed in some way by the teacher. He then tries to concentrate the learner's attention upon each of the constituents and to teach these in serial fashion. At first sight this common practice seems to be opposed to the equally common theory. It is usually held that we learn bodily skill by a series of more or less blind shots, and never really understand exactly how any such efficiency is acquired. We are told, for example, that if a man examines "his experience in learning an act of skill, he will recognise that to a large extent he did not foresee the favourable variations by which his movements became better. Nor did he recognise with any degree of clearness how the improvement was made after it came."[1] No doubt this is true, but it does not follow that the best method of attaining motor skill is merely one of relatively blind "trial and success."

[1] Freeman : *How Children Learn*, London, 1919, 132. Quoted by Pear, 37.

57

If this method were genuinely the best one to use, we ought never to attempt to train skilled movement. We ought simply to tell a man the sort of result he is expected to attain and then leave him to find his own way to this result. We cannot do this, even in the case of the athletic genius. The genius in skilled movement, like the genius in other fields, is the man who is continually experimenting with what he has been taught, whereas the ordinary man is satisfied with what he has been taught. When a genius finds a new way, he very often takes a long time to discover how he did it. He may never discover this. But if he does, provided his method is not entirely peculiar to his own bodily mechanism, it soon tends to become a part of what other people are taught.

Why is it, then, that the process of learning motor skill commonly appears to be haphazard and blind? It is because by far the greater part of skill in movement consists in fitting together rather elementary bodily activities, and little or none in the acquisition of some new, single, isolated movement. With movements, as with everything else that is part of life, when a number of them are fitted together, some novel, unforeseen and hitherto unknown result is apt to occur. The skilled man always knows the basic movements, and if he is to control and use his skill intelligently he must be able to picture, or think out, or at least carry out new ways of putting them together. But he can practically never accurately foretell what will result. And when the result is secured, not only the performance as seen from outside, but the feel of it by the performer, is apt to seem novel and hard to track to its source. However, this certainly does not mean, as some say, that it is no use trying to find out how first-class skill is acquired, but only that the effort to discover is a hard one, and that it must never stop short at describing the basic or constituent motions, but must be particularly concerned with how these movements are combined. Obviously the more a trainer is concerned with concerted skill, where many people have to act together—as is the case to a high degree in an army—the more important do these considerations become.

The basic movements may be known, however, and due attention may be paid to the way in which they have to be combined into a neat and "single" performance, and yet little advance may be made unless a trainer carefully considers the ways in which both of these may best be assimilated by the learner or the group of learners. Here we approach an extremely interesting but little explored field of psychological investigation.

A simple experiment may be used in order to help to define the problems involved. Suppose a number of people are placed before a screen; they are told that when the screen is removed they will see a long, narrow room with a chalk mark drawn across the floor of the room at a distance of about seven yards. They are to move forward at once and come to a halt with their toes exactly on this line.

They will have to step over a small obstacle before they reach the chalk mark. The people are then kept for a few moments, and thereupon, instead of the screen's being removed, they are simply asked to say what they have been experiencing, or how they have been thinking, during the period of delay. Some, probably, will say that all the time they were *picturing* what was on the other side of the screen ; that they could, in their mind's eye, see the room, the floor, the chalk mark, some kind of an obstacle, and very likely themselves walking towards the mark. Others will say that they felt "all of a tingle" to begin ; that they were taking up just the posture from which to start; that it was as if they were already making the movements that they were really only anticipating. Yet others may say that they were chiefly aware of going over in their mind the exact instructions given to them, and of seeming to hear them again and again. Others may report combinations of all of these processes. In any normal group there will also be people, always unsatisfactory to a psychologist, who are not able to say anything definite at all.

This simple experiment may help to demonstrate what is called "dominant imagery." One man makes a mental picture of what he has to do, and we say he belongs to a "visual type." Another feels as if his body is actually carrying out what he is expecting to do, and we say he belongs to a "kinaesthetic type." Another repeats to himself in words what is required of him, or may seem to hear the instructor repeating the words to him again, and we call this type in general "vocalising," though the words may appear as visual, auditory or motor images.

Professor Pear has made the brilliant and interesting suggestion that in the individual training of any complex form of motor skill we ought always to be on the look-out for the learner's dominant type of imagery and build our method upon that. The visualiser should *see* what is expected of him, be given pictures, models, diagrams, cinematographic films, and as often as possible watch the actual performances of qualified skilled people. The vocaliser should be given very careful descriptions, oral and written, and set to study these. The kinaesthetic type should learn by doing. In this last case a further distinction should be made between "putting through" and "active performance." In "putting through" a learner's movements are guided, he himself remaining relatively passive. In "active performance" the learner is all the while trying for himself under supervision. So far as experimental evidence goes, it appears that "putting through" is of comparatively slight value, at least in the learning processes of animals and young children, though there is some conflict of opinion upon this matter. The method may be more useful with a fairly intelligent type of adult, and particularly so when consistent and connected attention is given to the different *positions* taken up by the limbs concerned in the course of their movements, especially at points where the direction of movement changes.

The suggestion that a good method of training in muscular performance should follow a person's dominant imagery is a good one, but it requires far more careful experimental testing than it has yet received. It is, for example, probable that the best way of stimulating dominant imagery is almost always indirect, although a direct method may be necessary to help a person to *form* the imagery which he will later use. Thus a visualiser will visualise most definitely, not when he is stimulated by a direct visual method, as by the use of pictures, but when some other mode of teaching, not immediately suited to a visual method, is adopted. This puts him into a difficulty, and he will then fall back upon the mental pictures which give him help. In general, images are evoked only when some necessary reaction is delayed, as in our illustration of the screen and the chalk mark, or when some actual difficulty of adjustment is met with. For the present the best procedure in dealing with individuals is, first to find out the learner's dominant imagery,[1] if he has any, then to provide a basis for the formation of correct images by the use of some direct method—pictorial for the visualiser, verbal for the vocaliser, aided performance for the kinaesthetic type—and finally to stimulate the occurrence of images during the training process proper by the use of some indirect method. Meanwhile the

[1] Several ways of doing this are usually described in any good text-book of experimental psychology, but it should be admitted that current methods stand greatly in need of improvement.

major part of army training in this direction is group training, and until it becomes easy to sort out all men of a particular type and put them together, individual differences in any considerable group are such that an efficient instructor must put into operation all the methods available : the picture method, the description method, and some form of the kinaesthetic method. But he will not expect all individuals to profit equally from each method.[1]

[1] These suggestions are derived mainly from an unpublished piece of research carried out by Mrs L. C. Ramsey at the Cambridge Psychological Laboratory. The work was done with the aid of a grant from the Industrial Fatigue Research Board. There is great need for further experiments. The whole subject is attractive and promising, but very complex.

Chapter V. PRACTICE AND MOTIVES IN
LEARNING BODILY SKILL

Iт is important that both the teacher and the learner
of bodily skill should know something about the
normal effects of practice. Ordinary observation
teaches us that skill is rarely acquired by a regular
progression. Periods of improvement alternate with
periods during which the learner makes no progress
or even appears to lose some of the skill which he
seemed to have gained. Accurate information as to
the common results of practice may relieve a teacher
of much unnecessary irritation, and a learner of much
unnecessary depression or unjustifiable elation.

The subject has been extensively studied for
various relatively simple kinds of skill. The accuracy
and efficiency of a movement can often be measured
indirectly in terms of the amount of work done,
while in other cases a direct experimental record of
accuracy can easily be made. When a record of this
kind is kept, we can plot a curve showing how accuracy and efficiency increase with practice. Broadly
speaking, there are three common types of "work
curve" for muscular effort. In every case the improvement is irregular, but while in one type the
most rapid advance is made in the early stages of
practice, in another improvement is slow at first but
accelerates until the limit is reached, and in a third
the rate of improvement is relatively constant over

the whole of a long practice period. The first type seems particularly to mark the cases in which an old movement is being applied, with very little change, to a new situation. The second is that in which a more or less complex set of movements have to be reorganised in a radical manner. The third is rare except in the experimental laboratory, and applies for the most part only to simple mechanical movements in which practically all that happens is an increase in the speed of reaction, and not a re-conditioning or re-organisation of the action itself. These characteristic effects of practice vary not only with the type of task which has to be performed, but also with the individual, and are comparatively persistent for a given individual, within the limits of the type of muscular skill he has to perform.

With all fairly complex activities, however, there is another yet more important characteristic which the study of learning-curves brings out. This is the occurrence of what are commonly called *periods of plateau*. In learning a complex bodily activity, not only is there rapid acceleration of improvement at some points and a definite falling off of ability at others, but these two processes have a definite relationship. Thus a period in which there appears to be no progress or actual decline is followed immediately by a spurt upwards in performance value. And the total work curve may take on a form something like a series of steps. The flat portions, before the sudden spurts, mark periods of *plateau*.

This appears to occur largely because learning complex movements involves two different processes. First there is learning to make the movements themselves. While this is being done, as a rule the learner must give careful attention to each constituent movement. But in the second place all these movements have to be linked together and so organised that they may take on some of the characteristics of a habit. A high degree of skill in any complicated task always means that a large series of different movements have become relatively habitual. A habitual series is always one which goes on to a large degree outside the field of conscious attention. Not only so, but that organisation of movements which skill of any kind demands seems also to be a process that is perfected largely outside the field of conscious attention. It is not merely that rest renders the learner more capable of vigorous effort, but that during inactivity in a given direction the organisation of movements in that direction is positively improving. This is an illustration of how active tendencies, which operate outside of conscious attention, are continually producing important effects in the shaping of human behaviour. A tendency to organise certain movements, or an interest in the organisation of certain movements, is set up by conscious and directed effort. The *conscious* effort lapses, but the tendency still carries on, and produces its effects when we are not thinking of those effects at all.[1]

[1] On the other hand, some observers say that the periods of *plateau* represent unnecessary pauses and could be safely elimi-

There are three highly important practical conclusions which immediately follow from these considerations:

1. When any complicated form of bodily skill is being learned, both instructor and student must realise that periods during which no progress appears to be made are perfectly normal.

2. In order that any complex series of bodily movements should be given a fair chance to be consolidated, or organised, very persistent and prolonged repetition should be avoided.

3. The positively beneficial effects of distributed practice may continue to increase—in the usual step-wise manner—for longer periods than is commonly believed.

The second of these conclusions is bound up with the interesting and difficult problem of becoming "stale." I shall discuss this later, in connexion with the study of fatigue.

A related question of no small practical interest is the very disputed point whether, in teaching skill, attention should be concentrated first upon accuracy or first upon speed. Most instructors perhaps think that there is no question here at all. They say: "It is easier to speed up than to correct inaccurate movements." But this is less obvious than it looks.

It may be plausibly argued that a mere consideration of the mechanics of the moving parts of the

nated with proper teaching. There is not sufficient evidence to prove this point at present. The whole matter should be further studied.

body shows that a slow movement and a quick movement of the same limb cannot follow the same path. We may take one point only. It is easy to measure the speed at which a limb moves from one point to another over the whole of its path, and to show that this speed is never regular. There is acceleration after the initial impulse has set the limb moving, and deceleration before the limb comes finally to rest. The relative change of speed is not the same in quick as it is in slow movement, and coincidently with this change the path traversed is apt to be different. If we learn slowly and then speed up, we do more than speed up: we alter the path over which we carry out the movement. When, for example, a cricket coach makes a stroke very slowly for a beginner to see, he is not really doing just what he would do were he playing to a real bowler in a cricket match. There seems no doubt that all this is perfectly true, but its practical significance is less than has sometimes been maintained.[1]

Various experiments have been carried out to test the difference of opinion which exists at this point. I will briefly describe one, the results of which were fairly conclusive for the type of movements concerned.[2] Equal groups of children were taught typewriting, one by a speed method, another by an accuracy method. After equal

[1] See, e.g. Gilbreth: *Applied Motion Study*, New York, 1917, 109 ff.
[2] Sturt: 'Comparison of Speed with Accuracy in Learning Process,' *Brit. Journ. of Psychol.* vol. xii. 289–300.

amounts of practice, the speed group was told that it must be accurate, the accuracy group that it must work at top speed. In the result the two groups came very closely together indeed. Thus: " Between the two methods employed—(*a*) exclusive attention to speed, (*b*) exclusive attention to accuracy —there seems little to choose when considered simply as methods of learning. The choice must depend on other considerations, e.g. on how soon it is desired to use the product." If this conclusion is right, it seems probable that such change in the path of movement as may be necessary with speeding up is pretty easily acquired, and is in fact made unwittingly; the person concerned, that is, makes the adjustment required without thinking anything about it. The same experiment also strongly supported the conclusion that "a high quality of work can be obtained finally without insisting upon a high quality constantly throughout the learning process." This is obviously important for an instructor to bear in mind.

Finally I propose to turn away for a while from this experimental field of study, and to deal with the very difficult and little investigated question of the exact psychological motives underlying the acquisition of muscular skill. No really complicated bodily skill can be attained without prolonged effort. Once the skill is acquired, its main mark may be the apparently effortless way in which it is carried out, but, save in very exceptional circumstances indeed, the ease which marks a good performance has to be acquired as slowly, and with as much effort and as much persistence in repetition as the "good" performance itself. As the existence of *plateau* periods shows, there are, indeed, many stages on the way to completely skilled performance in which advance demands the suspension of conscious and detailed effort, but there is no doubt whatever that at other times—and they represent the greater part of the time—definite voluntary effort must constantly be made if improvement is to be effected.

Whenever persistent effort is maintained, there must obviously be some strong driving activity in operation. And the driving activity has to be attached just to those movements which the person is trying to perfect, or to some further end which by means of those movements he anticipates that he will secure. Motive is another name for this driving activity.

A distinction is often made between motives in play and those in work activities. In play, it is said,

especially in games which exercise the kinaesthetic and cutaneous organs, the motive for continuing is the pleasure the individual has in the movements he performs. For in many games, and even in some forms of work, muscular skill may express itself through patterns of bodily structure and bodily control closely related to instinctive patterns. The straightforward joy...which some adults find in games seems thus comprehensible. For such players games are activities motivated by instinct, and require for their continuance neither voluntary attention nor acts of will to prolong the effort. The predominant motive is (the) interest (of the performer) in the pleasures which he derives from his kinaesthetic sensations. It seems reasonable to call this *muscular sensitive-*

ness. And just as the other senses have stimulated persons whose enjoyment of them is epicurean, there are epicures of muscular sensation. Such fortunate people, enjoying not merely the sensations themselves but their higher groupings and patterns, are probably to be found among ballet dancers, figure skaters, swimmers, gymnasts and acrobats.[1]

A great part of this is undoubtedly true, but the capacity to find a sufficient spur in the sensations that arise from the production of bodily movements for continuing and perfecting such movements is rare. Moreover, when it does occur, it is probably much more closely connected with the maintenance of posture than with the actual production of movement.

I shall therefore discuss briefly certain common incentives which are outside the chains of bodily activities that have to be learned. These, that is to say, may be regarded as operating whatever may be the appreciation or lack of appreciation of the sensations which movements actually initiate.

No doubt the commonest of all these is some form of money payment. In one way the whole structure of modern society may be said to be arranged so as to enforce the importance of incentives arising from money. Thus, outside certain athletic performances, and even to a large extent inside them, the commonest of all the ways used to entice people to make the prolonged effort necessary for them to attain a high degree of muscular skill is to offer them

[1] Burnett and Pear : 'Motives in Acquiring Skill,' *Brit. Journ. of Psychol.* vol. XVI. 77–85.

valuable monetary rewards. But obviously enough, save in abnormal cases, it is not the possession of money, but what money can obtain, that gives to the wage, or the bonus, its strong driving force. This again depends upon the psychological fact that a normal man's activities or interests are not isolated and separated from one another, but are all organised together. Thus when a man, in order to get food or to buy books, tries hard to become a skilled artisan, it is not that the energy required for his bodily activities has literally borrowed some of the energy involved in food-seeking or in the pursuit of an intellectual interest, but that skill in movement, the satisfaction of bodily necessity and the pursuit of an intellectual interest have all been organised together. This at once places a limitation upon the use of the money incentive. In proportion as a man's instinctive tendencies and acquired interests are already satisfied, the stimulating effects of higher wages diminish. The typical situation in which money can be used to increase skill is where the ordinary money rewards offered are insufficient to maintain a standard of living which is conventional within the group concerned. It is not too much to say that if economic justice means that all the individuals belonging to a given community can, in the ordinary course of their wage-earning activities, secure just so much money as will enable them to satisfy the standard of life current in that community, then money can be used as an aid to higher efficiency only at the expense of economic injustice. In concrete terms, for example, suppose a good "shot" is paid better than an average "shot," this increased reward will promote efficiency only so long as the average reward falls somewhat below what is required to satisfy current standards of life.

There is another psychological effect which tends to make money not a very efficient incentive. This also is bound up with our present social order. When a man by increased monetary reward attains a standard of living somewhat higher than that of most of his fellows, this not only satisfies his present needs more effectively, but it at once develops new needs which must be met by yet greater rewards. Consequently the stimulating effects of differential reward for skill are apt to be very fleeting, and before long the limits of its effect in the production of more skilled movement are soon reached.

Finally the money incentive, like every other outside stimulus, is hindered by the process of "adaptation," as it is commonly called. Whenever any stimulus is continued unchanged for a length of time, we tend to get adapted to it, so that its stimulating effect almost automatically ceases. It is not necessary to discuss here the mechanism by which this result is produced. As to the result itself there is no possible dispute. A continuous sound soon ceases to be consciously heard, a continuous colour to be seen, and so on. Similarly a wage rate, or any rate of reward, very soon ceases to be regarded as of particular note, is accepted as a matter of course, and no longer produces its effects in stimulating unusual efforts unless it is still further increased.

Personal ambition, once it can be aroused, is undoubtedly a more inherently powerful motive or incentive to performance than is monetary reward. But it is not easy to produce a social environment in which it can operate as a genuinely widespread factor. For the effectiveness of personal ambition depends in most cases upon a society in which there are important differences of social ranking or of social authority. And it operates powerfully only so far as there can be a clear chance of personal advancement open to all the individuals concerned. Such chances are in practice not only bound to be limited, but also must be restricted in their range. So when an obvious limit has been reached, the incentive of personal ambition either ceases to operate or its end is changed. No doubt it is the practical difficulties in the way of constructing a social organisation, in which efficiency is the direct result of personal ambition, that have led to the adoption of fixed schemes of promotion such as advancement by seniority. And meanwhile the establishment of all such schemes works in a way directly against the incentive of personal ambition, and makes the acquisition of skill as a result of this rather the exception than the rule.

If the operation of personal ambition is perhaps rare and restricted, group tradition and some form of social competition are extraordinarily easy to arouse and are very efficient incentives, for they can be particularly readily combined with what the members of the group can actually do better than the members of other groups. Perhaps we touch here upon an incentive which is specially closely related to the Anglo-Saxon character. I shall have to deal with this more fully in connexion with a discussion of the important place in social organisation that may be taken by organised group or team games. But it is clear at once that if tradition is to be built up *on* efficiency, it demands the maintenance of efficiency if it is to be carried on. The question then is how the ordinary, perhaps somewhat stupid, member of an army unit can be moved by group tradition. To this question I shall return later. At present I merely wish to record my conviction that this factor of tradition and group competition is in practice the most psychologically satisfactory form of incentive to skilled bodily performance that we are able to use.

Such incentives apart, no doubt a great spur to a learner's impulse to succeed comes normally from the teacher. It often falls to his lot to have to apply the somewhat violent form of stimulus without which a lazy or uninterested individual or group will do nothing. A capacity for lurid language and violence of threat may be useful and even necessary in order to make a beginning. But this sort of initial impulse never by itself goes very far in the production of skill. The initial impulse having been given, recourse must be had to one or more of the relatively permanent incentives already discussed. Still the teacher remains important, however. Undoubtedly "most strikingly good performances involving muscular skill have been learned from a teacher."[1] It seems certain that in general even a poor teacher is better than none at all. This is probably because in any social situation suggestibility is apt to be heightened. The more suggestible a person is the more frequently does he accept ideas, or adopt movements, or experience feelings without any attempt to criticise himself in doing these things. Thus the place of the teacher is especially important in the early stages of acquirement of skill, when the question is rather that of the right lines to be adopted than of the exact movements which produce the greatest efficiency. There are two things, however, apart from the important temperamental factors involved, which may paralyse training. One is inefficiency on the part of an instructor—a point recognised by everybody. The other—much less generally recognised, but probably a much greater stumbling-block—is extreme and unveiled efficiency on the part of an instructor. A man more often gives up trying because his teacher is too expert than because he is not expert enough.

[1] Burnett and Pear: *op. cit.* 83.

Chapter *VI*. THE STUDY OF FATIGUE

Everybody has remarked that increasing fatigue means in general diminishing quality and quantity of work. It is also widely recognised that a fatigued group is, as a rule, one in which discontent prevails, and there is apt to be lowered *morale*. In war there is perhaps no general condition which is more liable to produce a large crop of nervous and mental disorders than a state of prolonged and great fatigue. For these and other reasons the study of fatigue— how it is caused, what are its results and how it may be counteracted—is a matter of very great importance to every military officer.

Fatigue may be defined as a state produced by repeated activity, whether bodily or mental, as a result of which the capacity for continuing a given activity is reduced unless special efforts are made. Comparatively little is known of the precise physiological and psychological character of the fatigued state. An important part of it, where bodily activities are concerned, has to do with the chemical and physical changes which take place in an active muscle; but under ordinary every-day conditions a far more important part has to do with the distribution of the nerve impulses upon which coordinated and well-regulated bodily activity depends. Resting muscle-fibres secrete a store of material in the form of glycogen. This, when a suitable stimulus is applied, breaks down into lactic acid, carbon dioxide and so on, and with this change there proceeds the contraction of the muscle, and the production of heat and certain electrical changes. "Thus, regarded as a machine, striated muscle is comparable to an internal combustion engine, the fuel of which not only provides the energy but also directly drives the mechanism".[1] With continued muscular activity, however, not only may the stored "fuel" be used up more rapidly than it can be replaced, but the chemical changes which accompany contraction may directly clog the efficient working of the muscle, and so lead to diminished output of work. Under normal working conditions, outside of special laboratory arrangements, as soon as ever this state of muscular fatigue threatens to approach, the worker more or less automatically effects a slight change of posture, the effect of which is to throw the strain of the work upon a somewhat different set of muscles, or to alter the rhythm of muscular contractions, or in some way to vary the distribution of energy expenditure throughout the muscular systems involved. The exact mechanism by which this change in muscular activity is brought about has yet to be made clear. But beyond question it is in the main the concern of the central nervous system, which controls the distribution of the nerve impulses that act as final stimuli for the production of muscular contraction. Thus it may well be the case that we

[1] C. S. Myers, *Industrial Psychology in Great Britain*, London, 1926, 39.

ought to look for the signs of oncoming fatigue, not to diminished output of work directly, but to a more than normally rapid change of posture, or to breaks in an established rhythm of muscular contraction, or, in the more extreme cases, to involuntary interpolations into a series of muscular contractions of irrelevant movements. Fatigue may then mean not so much a directly diminished capacity to carry out a given task as increased liability to be led away to the performance of other tasks.

It is perhaps worth trying to put all this in a more concrete way. Imagine a man occupied upon some muscular work such as digging a trench or shovelling away a mound of earth. There are perhaps half a dozen or more ways in which he can carry out his task efficiently. He works in one way for a time, then slightly shifts his grip of the tool, or his stance, and carries on. He rings the changes upon his various slightly differing methods fairly regularly and with a more or less constant rhythm. But a time comes when the changes become more sporadic, less regular, more rapid perhaps. Fatigue is threatening him. Further, any man at work has a certain one job upon which he is centred. But all the time stimuli are pouring in upon him, through his eyes, his ears, his skin, his mouth and throat and all the various avenues of sense perception, which invite him to do other jobs. These stimuli are not very effective at first; they become more and more effective. It is not that he literally *could* not work at his one central job, so far as the muscular apparatus which does that job is concerned, but that more and more he is trying to do a lot of different jobs at once, and so the central job suffers. Then also we call him "fatigued".

There is another matter of high practical importance in relation to fatigue study, though it has received less experimental treatment than it deserves. Any man who is engaged upon a relatively mechanical or routine type of work, whether muscular or mental, has normally to strike a balance between whatever it is that keeps him at his job and various other tendencies that are constantly seeking expression in his life. Nobody normally does only one thing at a time, although, as we have just seen, everybody normally has one task with which he is at a given time most immediately concerned. A man works, and in proportion as his work is of a routine and mechanical character, he also talks, or sings, or whistles, or hums, or dreams, or in default of anything else falls into a state of pleasing semi-somnolence. All this is well, so long as the balance is maintained; but it can be readily toppled over, one way or the other, and then, either way, the work is apt eventually to suffer. For example, the very great value of music as an accompaniment of any form of routine and particularly repetitive work has often been commented upon. Usually this value is said to consist in the aid given by music to the establishment of rhythms of performance. It is unquestionably more than this. It may, in fact, give just that balance between stimuli to work and "other stimuli" which any ordinary group of workers needs if work is to be efficient and relatively free from fatigue.

All these factors—the sequence of postures, the maintenance of rhythm, the co-ordination of movements, the balance between stimuli to the work and other stimuli—are a matter less of the state of local muscles than of the distribution of nerve impulses, and they play predominant parts in most cases of what is ordinarily called "fatigue".

It may appear that the discussion has, so far, been rather unduly theoretical. Not only is every part of it, however, based upon a very considerable amount of experimental research, but it at once opens up the most important practical points in regard to the regulation of normal working conditions so as to avoid undue fatigue. As any worker will recognise, there is rarely or never any complex bodily activity which can be carried out in one single "best" way only. There are a number of "good" ways, a number of efficient ways, and in doing the work and at the same time keeping fresh a man will involuntarily, or unwittingly, shift from one to another of these ways when the working spell is at all prolonged. It should be the concern of anybody who is in charge of workers to observe these shifts—of posture, of sequence of movements, of stress of a given component movement and the like—and to organise them so that the change from one to another is facilitated. Everybody now recognises the importance of rhythm— the grouping and proper emphasis of the component movements of a body series—in muscular work. In the army, in particular, rhythm in routine performances is constantly and rightly prescribed and demanded. But insistence upon a single rhythm, in long-continued work, may be as mistaken as entire neglect of the rhythmic character of efficient muscular activity. There is a rhythm of the general bodily "set", or posture, or attitude, which is just as important as the rhythm of component muscular contractions; and if I am right, it is in changes in the normal sequence of the former rhythm that the earliest signs of fatigue are apt to appear. Thus our discussion issues in certain practical conclusions which may now be formulated:

1. In attempting to organise any form of continued muscular performance, first try to observe carefully the changes in posture, attitude, and general body-set which are illustrated in a normal efficient performance throughout a working spell.

2. These changes should be encouraged and as far as possible organised. To prohibit them in the interests of an unvarying uniformity is a profound mistake. A working man always has a far greater variety of efficient performances than a working machine.

3. Be especially on the look-out for any signs of a marked change in these periodic "shifts" from one way of work to another, and particularly for any increase in their rapidity. Such marked change probably means that the bounds of a satisfactory working spell have been overpassed.

Here we approach two questions the study of which has produced a great quantity of experimental enquiry. These are: the best length of a working spell and the best length of a rest period. Hardly any profitable generalisation is possible. Very broadly speaking, it is true that relatively short working spells, with short rests, are more economical than long spells of work with longer rest periods. For example: "In heavy muscular work, in work involving mental strain, and in light repetitive and monotonous work the efficiency of a spell of work which exceeds four hours can be improved if divided into two halves separated by a few minutes' pause".[1] But each occupation must be studied by itself with a view to determining the most efficient distribution of work and rest. What is important is to realise that both of these, as in the case of the rhythm of movements in a given performance and of body-set throughout a whole working period, are capable of profitable organisation. For each type of task there appears to be a work period which is better than any other, and there is a rest pause which is just long enough to maintain the freshness and keenness of the worker and not so long that he loses that incitement and ease which come as work at any task proceeds.

It is hardly necessary, perhaps, to point out that the individual variations as regards the best working and rest periods must be fully recognised. There are, for example, some persons who always work best in

[1] Myers, *op. cit.* 64.

short and violent spurts with many brief rests, and others, equally adapted by natural or acquired ability for the task in hand but temperamentally different, who do better with long work periods and fewer but longer rests. As far as possible such facts as these ought always to be considered in making up a squad or gang of men for working purposes.

Even when the greatest care is taken in the organisation of methods of work and in settling work and rest periods, the performances, as measured by output, never for long remain uniform. Indeed if they do the general inference to be drawn is that the men who are at work are not going "all out", or nearly "all out". It is, of course, often possible to measure output at regular intervals over the whole of a working period—whether of an hour, a day, a week or a much longer time—and then, plotting amounts produced against time, to arrive at a "work curve". With work involving considerable muscular fatigue such curves tend to fall towards the end of a morning's work, to recover after midday, and then to fall progressively and decisively during an afternoon's spell. If the work is less physically heavy, but makes demands upon skill and dexterity, the curve tends to rise slowly during the morning spell to a maximum, then to decline somewhat, to show less complete recovery than in the case of violent muscular effort, and finally to fall again less decisively in the afternoon. Again, if the movements involved in the work are of a marked rhythmical character, there tends to be a considerable rise during the morning, and thereafter, save with excessive hours of work, a well maintained level throughout the day.

If the views which were put forward in the early part of this chapter are sound, nearly all work may be regarded as involving a state of balance between responses to stimuli which are directly productive of a given effort and responses to other stimuli presented at the same time. Except, perhaps, with exceedingly simple tasks and in abnormal cases, none of us ever merely does only one thing. If we could fully express, say, the work-patterns of a navvy, we should find them made up of far more than the sensations and percepts coming from the touch and sight of his tools, the appearance of the bank of earth he was at work on, of the trolley he was filling and the like. An integral part of the pattern would come from many other sources: what his pals were saying, the touch of his clothes, his desire for a pipe, the sound of a tune whistled and so on. These would be found not to be merely indifferent to his efficiency, but they would directly influence it positively or negatively. Now anybody who is concerned to maintain efficiency in human activity without fatigue must be alive to these "extra" elements in a general work-pattern. He must consider what combinations fit together, and what hinder one another. Here is a great field for further observational and experimental work. It is well known, for example, that relatively mechanical types of response in laboratory experiments tend to become both more

efficient and less tiring when a subject falls into a
state of sleepy day-dreaming, and conversely that
the latter state is facilitated by the former type of
response. But such relationships of "work activities"
and "other activities" need to be discovered in wider
fields. Perhaps it is an exaggeration to say that the
main secret of avoiding fatigue—so far as it can be
avoided—lies in finding the right sort of "other
activity". But such a statement is, I think, at least
an exaggeration in the right direction.

Some problems of great importance arise in connexion with the relation of fatigue to the relatively
intensive physical training to which a recruit in the
army is often subjected. The whole force of our
discussion so far has tended to show that fatigue
cannot be successfully counteracted by the development of large and strong local muscles. By far the
greatest emphasis under normal conditions has to be
placed upon training in the regulation and co-ordination of movements, that is, upon the effective
co-operation of the central nervous system with the
various muscles involved.

Before the late war it was observed that German
recruits in the early stages of their training generally
lost weight. After about three months they gained
weight again, but the gain was due mainly to a
development of leg muscles brought about chiefly
by marching exercises. The arm muscles remained
pretty constant, while those involved in breathing
processes actually fell off in volume. Now a big
muscle is very rarely a resistant muscle. Mosso

showed long ago that while big muscles may enable a man to hoist up, say, a heavy weight once, they are much less efficient when it is a question of lifting a small weight a large number of times. Very often the stage "strong man" is of all people the least able to make such continuous efforts as are demanded in many ordinary industrial occupations, or in numerous common military evolutions.

Leitenstorfer,[1] a German military doctor, carried out a long series of observations of a certain battalion which was famous for the degree of perfection to which its men were trained. He found a number of cases of heart trouble, particularly of dilatation of the heart, due to over-exercise, and a large number of instances of acceleration of pulse-beat during rest. In manœuvres the battalion not only showed up very badly, but was beaten by another battalion which had been far less highly trained. The observation is not an isolated one, and the moral is plain. Mere muscular training is of little use, and may be a positive disadvantage. It is capacity for resistance that must be trained. This means that all the while stress must be laid upon the proper distribution of effort, not upon the making of sudden big spurts in a dramatic fashion. Training must be as varied as possible, and the periods of training ought not to be unduly prolonged. It is easier to acquire big muscles than to learn ease of movement, but the latter is more important. In this connexion it is interesting to notice that an acquired bodily ability

[1] Quoted from J. Ioteyko, *La Fatigue*, Paris, 1920, 140-1.

87

which can be performed easily and skilfully can be kept from deteriorating with a small amount of regular practice, and can be retrained, as a rule, with considerable speed.

Overtraining, leading to fatiguability, must be distinguished from "staleness". The latter, as it is generally understood, concerns not a training period proper, but a peculiar state of inefficiency which follows upon frequently repeated exercise after the training proper is completed, or at least after its early periods are over. A skilled performer suddenly finds that he can do nothing right. He is not, so far as he can tell, specially tired. He can make the required efforts readily enough. He has as lively a desire as ever to do well. But nothing goes the right way. A whole group may be affected together, or, one member of a group becoming "stale" in this way, his state may, by the infection of suggestion, at once spread to the rest.

"Staleness" raises psychological problems of too great complexity for them to be fully discussed here. In some cases, no doubt, it merely means that an individual or a group has reached a *plateau* period. In effect the organism is crying out: "Leave me alone. Let me do my work by myself. Don't force me". Then, once the "stale" period is over, there is a spurt upwards in performance.

In other cases "staleness" undoubtedly means that the necessary balance of "other activities" has been somehow upset. The individual or group has centred too exclusively upon the one performance,

ignoring the peculiar fact that all efficient performance, if it is to be continued, must have a compensating
balance of other performances apparently not immediately connected with the central achievement.
If the need for these other performances is not
recognised, a time comes when the demand for
them is so great that it produces incoordinated
movement, conflicting—though the performer may
all the time remain unaware of the source of the
trouble—with the main task in hand.

In other cases what is called "staleness" is largely
a temperamental disturbance brought on by a shift
of mood, and often preceded by some abnormally
poor or abnormally good performance. The performer loses his self-confidence, becomes depressed,
and goes from bad to worse. Or he may be unduly
elated and rest upon his achievement.

A thorough psychological survey of "staleness"
has yet to be made. Though it be called by the same
name, it may undoubtedly have many and varied
causes and may have to be dealt with in various
different ways. The *plateau* type calls for rest. The
over-balanced type, as it might be called, demands
the provision of coincident and appropriate compensating responses. The *temperamental* type can
often be combated if external circumstances can be
so arranged that the performer can produce with
ease just that type of reaction needed to set off
the circumstances which induced his unfavourable
mood.

I have said nothing specifically about mental

fatigue. The reason for this is that mental fatigue in so far as it directly affects the ordinary soldier is mainly of importance in relation to nervous and mental disturbances. These will be dealt with later. Meanwhile it may be remarked that nobody has as yet produced unequivocal evidence for the occurrence of direct mental fatigue. In this field, especially, it seems certain that fatigue marks not directly decreased capacity to perform a given task, but an increased liability to harmful distraction which may, of course, produce the same practical result.

PART TWO

LEADERSHIP, DISCIPLINE AND MORALE

Chapter I. APPETITE AND INSTINCT GROUPS

U P to the present I have been concerned with some of the more technical problems of psychology, with problems that have been and are being investigated largely in the laboratory by the help of experimental methods. But an army is always primarily a fighting group. Its organisation and efficiency depend upon some of the most fundamental and powerful of human instincts ; and however much these may be supplemented and transformed by the growth of civilisation, they remain prominent and essential factors in military life. It is to problems directly connected with these that I now propose to turn. For their study we shall be bound, for the most part, to go outside the laboratory, and to try to understand the main motives underlying conduct in the general every-day life of the soldier. Some of the questions which I am going to discuss are : discipline, authority and punishment, the basis of leadership, the development of *morale*, and the causation and treatment of nervous and mental disease in warfare.

In every one of these cases a most important

question is how, exactly, a man may be influenced by membership of a group. Comparatively few of our most interesting occupations, if we except purely academic or purely literary and artistic efforts—and often not even with these exceptions—are carried out in solitude; and practically all the important occupations of military life have to be exercised in a group, or with reference to a group. A man inside a group and the same man outside the group are obviously in very different positions. Nothing influences us more profoundly or more subtly than the traditions, customs and general atmosphere of the groups to which we belong. A man who is timid, vacillating and indecisive when he is by himself may in a group be apparently brave, decisive, and single-minded. In fact, when people come together and form a group, each individual concerned may be capable of conduct of which no single member of the group would be capable if he were alone. The study of the influence upon individual conduct of membership of a group is what constitutes social psychology, and before we can take up the special practical questions which are now to be our main concern, we must consider a few of the leading principles which arise from a study of the psychological factors in group life.

Social psychology is best defined as the systematic study of how individual conduct is modified by membership of a group and by the interactions of groups. It is most important to remember that we have to deal not merely with the influence upon a

man of his membership of one group, but with the
ways in which different groups may be related
together. This is true not only because, as a matter
of fact, a man in the modern world is always at the
same time a member of various different groups,
but also because in nearly all, if not in all, cases,
whenever any new movement grows up inside a
group it is due to the contact of that group with
some other community.

It is necessary at this point to understand exactly
what constitutes a group in the psychological sense
of the word. Perhaps in ordinary conversation we
most frequently think of a group in territorial terms,
as a number of things or persons gathered together
within certain defined geographical boundaries. But
it is very hard to make any important psychological
use of such a territorial definition. In the modern
world, with its ease of communication and its
spreading of interests, some of the most important
and influential groups have no definite geographical
boundaries. There is, in fact, only one way in which
the human social group can be psychologically
defined, and that is by the agencies through which
it is organised. There are three outstanding facts
about any group that can be treated as a genuine
psychological unit. The first is that it is invariably
an *organisation*, not simply a collection, of persons.
The second is that the persons are held together by
some active bond of the nature of an "interest,"
which belongs not to their external environment,
but to their mental life. The third is that the group

must, in general, be regarded as functioning, as actually doing something both in relation to the individuals that belong to it and in relation to the social world of which it is a part.

Half a dozen people in a railway carriage, each buried in his own book or newspaper, or concerned with his own thoughts, are a mere collection, and not psychologically a group at all. But if one of the half dozen should begin to talk about some topic of prominent interest, a murder, a famous law-case, a much advertised sporting event, very likely the others will at once join in, and then they immediately become psychologically a group. They are now not merely together in a confined space, but they are consolidated, organised by a common interest. There are a number of tendencies belonging to the mental life of man which can thus organise groups. It is important to distinguish these, for they produce different types of social organisation and so lead to very different results in the way of individual conduct. The matter is of more than mere theoretical interest, for if we wish to understand the basis of discipline, the effects of punishment, the secrets of leadership, and the development of *morale*, we must know the type of group we have to deal with. I shall therefore put together into a concise definition all the ways in which a group can be psychologically organised :

A group is a collection of people organised by some common appetite, instinct, caprice, interest, sentiment, or ideal.

All groups which come early in social development are organised by appetite, by instinct, or by
some powerful but relatively temporary caprice. As
civilisation develops, the method of organisation of
the social group becomes continually more and
more complex. The old foundations of grouping
are, however, never completely lost. In times of
crisis, such as at the outbreak of war, there is
always a tendency for groups to revert to a rather
primitive stage in many of their characteristics.
Consequently we must take the appetite and instinct group first and ask what are its significant
general psychological characteristics.

In their intrinsic nature appetites are rhythmic,
seasonal, intermittent, and fluctuating. This is very
notably the case in their normal expression by the
higher animals and man. Man's hunger is not always
equally active; it is aroused after some period of
bodily activity, is satisfied, and sleeps again for a
while. Only the pathological, abnormal individual
is always thirsty. The same is true of the sex impulses, of the tendency to sleep, and in fact of all
appetites. Thus when a group is organised by
appetite, it is, if other factors are not all the time
coming in to help to hold it together, effective for
so long only as the appetite itself is awake and
active. Then, the appetite satisfied for the time
being, the group disintegrates. The same kind of
thing is true of the instinct group, though not for
quite the same reasons. Instinctive activity is always
largely a matter of external environment. There are,

as everybody now recognises, instinctive ways of meeting danger. But if the environment is regarded as a perfectly safe one, it goes without saying that these modes of response do not occur. Any group which is organised in the main by instinctive activity is always very much at the mercy of its environment. A marked change in this is apt to lead immediately to the disintegration of the group.

For example, every modern nation is a highly complex social unit, organised in many different ways and by many different agencies. But if it is suddenly threatened by war, it at once tends to revert to a more primitive stage and to become a group mainly organised by a few fundamental instinctive activities, all connected with meeting danger. At once many of the outstanding facts which characterise the grouping of the nation in times of peace fall away. But the change is a fleeting one. As soon as the danger passes, or as soon as the group becomes adapted to it, the instinctive activities again suffer control by those more lately acquired, and the social classifications which they directly produce cease to dominate all others.

The first important point, then, is that whenever a group is organised by appetite or instinct, it is apt to be highly unstable and liable to disintegration. In any lasting social organisation the appetite and instinct bonds must be reinforced by others.

In my definition of a group I said that the latter might be organised by a temporary strong caprice. This type of group is particularly interesting in

some ways, and is very frequently found in contemporary social life. But it will not concern us
directly, and, since I shall say little about it later,
I may make a few remarks concerning it here. If
a man keeps a watch upon his own conduct he will
constantly find that various "fads" seem suddenly
to appear, to run their course for awhile, and then
to drop completely away. There is often no obviously clear reason for this. For example, he gets
some trick of expression which is always creeping
into his speech. He says with every other sentence
"and so on and so forth", and then suddenly drops
this phrase, and uses "et cetera" instead. Exactly
the same sort of whim, fashion, fancy, and fad hold
sway in social life. Nobody knows precisely where
they come from, or why they speedily become rife.
They run through whole groups of people. For the
time being they are a badge which holds the group
together, and are a symbol of comradeship, like red
ties, or Oxford trousers, or "Russian" boots. Undoubtedly the same kind of thing is to be found
in military circles: tricks of drill, fashions of dress,
dodges in musketry and so on. The groups that get
formed about and by these passing fashions are the
expressions of temporary caprice. Like the appetite
group, like the instinct group, they are unstable and
tend to pass swiftly, for the basis of their organisation is a shifting one.

There is a second important point about the
psychological nature of the appetite and instinct
group. This has to do with differences of rank in

society. In practically all the groups with which we are directly concerned grading into ranks is customary. Now the recognition of differences of rank comes very early in social development, though regularly graded ranking is a late invention. Within the appetite and instinct group rank is determined in the most direct way possible by the degree to which an individual possesses the appetite or instinct that takes the lead in organising the group as a whole. This at once gives us the most important reason for two facts that are frequently noticed about leadership. In all relatively lowly groups leaders are apt to occupy a more than usually insecure position. This is because the appetite or instinct controlling the group may wane and be replaced by others, or because the person who temporarily takes the lead is satisfied earlier than the majority of the members of the group, or for some other reason of that kind.

Then, again, it has often been pointed out that once a group is faced with a crisis, some other person or persons than the selected leader or leaders come uppermost. This is because a leader who is put into his position by others is not by any means necessarily the person who possesses to the highest degree the appetite or the instinctive activity which rules the group when it is faced with difficulty. The selected leader may then be deposed until the crisis passes away, whereupon he resumes his rank.

Finally, in any group that is organised chiefly by appetite or instinct, nonconformity is apt to be dealt with in a most summary manner. There is a whole-heartedness about the conduct of groups at this level which cannot brook opposition or singularity. When, in a hunting pack, an animal is wounded or distressed, so that it falls behind the others, often they turn upon it with "sudden deadly rage" and rend it to pieces. For the whole effectiveness of the group at this stage depends upon the maintenance of the dominant driving appetite or instinct. If this weakens, the group must fall apart. Thus singularity and nonconformity in behaviour attract attention and awaken furious opposition. This phenomenon also has its parallel in the society which we know directly. In the social group which, in face of special difficulties, tends to revert to an appetite or instinct type of organisation, the nonconforming individual meets with the utmost intolerance and with condign punishment. This fact, as we shall see, has important implications in relation to the question of the use of punishment in maintaining discipline.

Chapter II. INTEREST, SENTIMENT, AND IDEAL GROUPS

No society based solely or mainly upon appetite, instinct, or the pursuit of some temporary need can endure for very long. In the course of development, therefore, other organising agencies soon mingle with these earlier and more direct ones. There is an immediate psychological basis for this. No man is ever moved in all his behaviour by a single instinct or an isolated appetite. Thus the very same group, so far as its individual components go, which at one time is held together by hunger is at another consolidated by reaction to danger, or by pugnacity, or, it may be, by sex responses. This paves the way towards the specialisation of functions within a community. Sub-groups appear, each having its particular part to play in the general social life. A hunting band in the pursuit of its prey has to face danger. Thereupon the basis of its organisation may be changed ; the more pugnacious section comes temporarily uppermost. Soon it may be that yet another section gains prominence, a group of primitive priests, who perhaps do not themselves fight, but whose function it is to try to guard against the danger which the hunters and the warriors have to meet by the elaboration of some form of magical or religious ritual. The emergence of such groups marks a development of social life. They are not theoretically a part of the most primitive social order, though as a matter of fact there is no known group at the human level in which they are not found. They inevitably grow up, because no man and no group can be consistently dominated by a single tendency. This sub-grouping, and the specialisation of functions which goes with it, proceed to immense lengths in the modern world and produce the greater part of the almost bewildering complexity of social life as we know it. Such specialisation invades every realm of human effort. Groups occupied with special processes of material art come relatively early in the history of social development. Special sets of people concern themselves with house-building, with making canoes, basketry, pottery and so on. Each particular art tends to have its special group, which guards the secrets of that art, but very likely knows little of any other. The modern world goes, of course, far beyond that, specialises within each trade, and lets a man spend a whole lifetime upon one small part of some complex productive process. As we have repeatedly seen, this progress towards minute specialisation is prominently illustrated in the history of the growth of the modern army.

Now I propose to call all these specialised groups which grow up in the course of social development "interest groups". There are two main reasons for adopting this name. First, membership of such a group generally indicates in the person concerned the presence of a particular interest in whatever it is that the group does, and second, the term "interest," whenever it is used in psychological discussion, should refer to some mental factor which grows up as a result of development and is not to be regarded as a part of the original psychological mechanism of man. An interest group, then, is always a sub-group in a larger community, possessing specialised social functions and held together by some active tendency which has grown up through differentiation and combination of appetites and instincts.

One very important point immediately emerges. Since an interest group is always a part of a larger social organisation, a natural basis is provided for the growth of a certain degree of individual freedom. We have seen that nonconformity within the appetite or instinct group is very apt to be summarily killed. There is no appeal outside the group itself within which the nonconforming conduct is manifested. But with the development of the interest group the possibility of such an appeal is at once secured. An individual who does not conform to the requirements of his own specialised group may be scouted by his fellow-members. He can however, theoretically at any rate, appeal to the larger society of which his group is a part. Such an appeal is often made. It is the beginning of public justice and of the systematised application of punishment.

With the emergence of the interest group society

is beginning to learn the secrets of a permanence which is independent of the special appetites of the individuals who make it up, or of the instinctive activity which its environment arouses. The secret is that social control now passes partially outside the bounds of the psychological activity involved and becomes directly exercised by custom, institution, and tradition. There are some interesting psychological reasons why this should be so, but they are perhaps of a rather theoretical order, and I shall not discuss them here. It is sufficient to point out that within an interest group individual action *is* frequently controlled directly and to a high degree by custom and tradition. When, in an interest group, a large number of people observe the same custom, their individual attitudes are no doubt widely divergent, but all alike are being influenced by a common tradition. The force of tradition in social life is everywhere recognised. The more a man identifies himself with his group, the more conservative does he become in relation to the customs of that group. He may, of course be tremendously radical about the traditions of other groups, but the institutions of his own must be conserved. This tendency to keep certain things unaltered is a leading characteristic of many relatively primitive human groups. "As among all savage tribes," say Spencer and Gillen, "the Australian native is bound hand and foot by custom. What his fathers did before him, that he must do. If during the performance of a ceremony his ancestors painted a white line across the forehead, that line he must paint. Any infringement of custom, within certain limitations, is visited with sure and often severe punishment".[1] Very much the same is true of many more modern groups. Conservation is almost invariably heightened by society. This at once gives to the institution and the tradition a capacity for persistence which is independent of individual attitude or length of life, and of the external environment. The group now tends to centre on the institution rather than on appetite or instinct. It has achieved the secret of a persistent and continuous life by changing the main basis of its organisation. To take only one illlustration, within the appetite or instinct group it is the *leader* who counts, the first-class fighter, the particularly greedy person, or the abnormally vain. But in the interest group the power shifts to the *institution* of leadership. Hereditary leadership tends to make its appearance. A man who has no very outstanding personal capacity may yet prove capable of sustaining the lead because it is not now the leader so much as leadership itself which is influential. So in early tribal warfare fighters always made strenuous efforts to attack the chief. If he could be killed the battle was often as good as over. But this becomes less and less the case, since to kill a particular man is not to destroy leadership.

The development of the interest group, then, can at once be seen to have two important consequences. First, it increases individual freedom, for it provides

[1] *Native Tribes of Central Australia*, London, 1899.

a mechanism of appeal from the vengeance of one group to the mercy of another. Second, it ensures a more permanent and continuous social life, for it leads to the organisation of a group about institution, custom, and tradition.

An institution or a custom persists throughout a great variety of circumstances; but it may excite very different ideas and feelings at different times. War regalia, for example, are very differently regarded in war and in peace. In war they inspire pride, anger, pugnacity, and joy; in peace they may inspire disgust, or mere boredom, or curiosity and so on. Now whenever a number of feelings and emotions tend to get organised around a single object, we have what the psychologist calls the development of a "sentiment". Patriotism is a sentiment, so is duty, so is friendship. They all stand for a variety of emotional experiences, all having reference to a common object or idea. With the development of interest groups, sentiments tend to take a leading place in the determination of social conduct. Sentiments are stabilising and conserving forces. They draw their strength from past history. The sentiment-ridden man is least of all likely to do violence to the traditions of his group, and thus, although the interest group provides a mechanism of appeal from an adverse social judgment, that appeal is on the whole not very likely to be made. I shall return to the significance of this, especially in discussing the psychology of discipline.

The interest and sentiment groups are not, however, the last word in social development. On the whole they stress the differences between social sets. It is the special function that forms the group's rallying point. All the men of one trade come together into one group; all the men of another into a different group. Each special group may be well organised, but on the whole it is self-contained, intolerant of other groups, and somewhat narrow in its outlook. A further step is taken as different groups gain a common membership; for then various individuals, ruled in some respects by one set of customs, will be ruled in other respects by a different set. This at once facilitates the attempt to find common features in differing groups. The apparently divergent social functions may be reconciled, may be shown to lead towards much the same ends. Then the different groups tend to be built together by an deal, and the new, wider, ideal group is formed. Each group still maintains its own character and its own functions, only it is fully recognised that these are not necessarily antagonistic but may be complementary. An ideal group is a combination of interest groups on the basis of a general similarity of aim. I shall later show that the development of the ideal group has a very great influence upon the basis of social authority, the relation of punishment to discipline, the limits of individual freedom in the group, the conditions of stable social leadership, and particularly upon the foundation of *morale* in group life. All these points are, however, best brought out in their relation to concrete problems which an officer in the army must meet for himself.

I have now completed this brief survey of the different kinds of social group, and of some of their psychological implications. I attempted it because I wish to show that the status of the individual in the group, and how he should be treated, depend to a large extent upon how the group with which we are concerned is psychologically organised. Before I attack the specific question of discipline and its psychological nature there are two other general questions that must be considered. These are: the importance of a study of the contact of groups, and the limits to what an individual may accomplish in group life.

Chapter III. THE NATURE AND IMPORTANCE OF SOCIAL CHANGE

In this chapter I propose to discuss a matter which is of great practical and theoretical interest: the study of the importance and nature of social changes. Any genuinely active and effective group of men must be continually developing and perhaps changing its customs and institutions and building up new traditions. The group which merely carries on old and well-established ways never goes very far. There is no doubt that with the group, as with the individual, by far the greatest stimulus to change comes from outside, from other persons and from other groups. The more a group is cut off from contact with other groups, the more is it wholly wrapped up in its established customs and the less likely is it to progress and develop and to strengthen the bonds of its group life. The key-word of social progress is the blending of the customs, traditions, material art, beliefs, and practices of different groups. Within any group the power of conservation tends to be very great. But when one group comes into effective contact with another its ways of doing things, its cherished customs and its beliefs may receive a rude shock. For here are other customs, other practices, other beliefs equally as cherished as its own. The conflict between the two cultures which then ensues is beyond all doubt the greatest possible stimulus to social change.

There are, broadly speaking, two ways in which this interplay between groups takes place. The first is technically known as the "contact" of cultures, and the second as "borrowing".

In the first form a group migrates as a whole from its settled home taking with it its own peculiar customs and social institutions. It comes to rest in a new environment and in close relationship to a different group. The migrating group may come as friendly emigrants, or they may come as fighters to dispossess the natives, or they may come merely seeking a new home and willing, if they can find it, to keep as far as possible to themselves. However they come, the result is that different sets of social customs mingle and probably clash with one another, and there is much social change on both sides.

This form of development of social life has been carefully studied by ethnologists, who have been chiefly concerned with primitive people. There is little reason to doubt that among savage peoples it does form the most powerful means for the spread of culture. In the modern world the movement of groups as a whole is less common. It occurs of course in every large war, and in every well-organised effort of colonisation. What is known as "the white man's burden"—though it might nearly as well be called the "black man's burden"—is due directly to that contact of social customs and institutions which all modern colonisation involves.

In another way, however, contact between groups is exceedingly common in the world we know. A characteristic of modern society is the great increase which it makes possible in the number of sub-groups in a whole community. We have developed many ways by which such groups may be brought into contact, so that each may be influenced by the others. One of the most important of these is through the establishment of organised group games, on which I shall have more to say later.

The second method by which a group may be influenced from outside itself is known as "borrowing". Here we must picture, not a group moving as a whole, but a migrant individual who goes away from his group and lives for a while in an alien environment. He finds there certain customs, which he assimilates. Later he returns to his own group. He may continue the new practices ; more than that, he may try to introduce them to his native society. There they may take root and grow, and once more, though this time by a different mechanism, a social group has been stimulated and changed by influences coming from outside its own borders.

I have put the case theoretically and in general terms. The situation with which I am dealing is, however, a very common one, and of direct significance to us. An officer in the army is, to some extent at least, in charge of the social organisation of a group of men. He himself does not normally belong to exactly the same set, or sets, that they belong to. He comes to them with a different training, with different traditions, customs, beliefs, codes of behaviour and so on. If he is going to keep his group alive and effective, he cannot simply let them continue an unchanging routine. The group must move in tune with the rest of the social world, and he, as their officer, must take trouble to try to understand something about the way in which social movements spread from group to group, and about the different forms which they take.

What happens when two groups come into contact depends partly upon such factors as the relative numbers in each group, especially the relative numbers of the different sexes, the nature of the external physical environment, and the particular sphere of social culture which brings them together. I shall deal, however, only with more obviously psychological considerations, and by far the most important of these concern the nature of the social relationship displayed between the groups concerned. There are three important cases. First, one group may be markedly assertive and the other definitely submissive. Second, the two groups may be friendly and may mix without assertiveness on the one hand or submissiveness on the other. Third, both groups may be moderately assertive and moderately submissive. Perhaps the first of these is the most important for us to consider, for it is on the whole the relationship which most naturally goes with conquest.

When a very assertive and dominant group meets and vanquishes a submissive group, it may appear as if the culture of the latter is swept entirely away and replaced by that of the former. But social customs have an extraordinary power of persistence which it is hard completely to explain. It often happens that the culture of the submissive group is driven into secret, and in secret it continues. The social situation is a very unstable one, and the apparently vanquished reactions are apt to come back with a vengeance should any special time of crisis arrive. When a higher civilisation has forcibly replaced a lower one, if, for any reason, a revolution occurs, the outworn displaced customs may appear suddenly to surge back with the utmost brutality.

This situation is well illustrated in Torday's study of the Bushongo, a vigorous but much depleted Central African tribe.

Not half an hour from the town (Kinchasa) [he says] were native villages...where, although mixed to some extent with the worst of European culture, the life of the black man was the same as it had been before the advent of the white conquerors, with this main difference, that ceremonies clashing with the ideals of the new over-lord were now performed in secrecy instead of openly as before. There never was a fear of betrayal among the negroes: no man, a native of the place, would have "split" on another belonging to his race. If a crime were committed by a chief or a man of importance, and were found out by the authorities of the Congo State, some volunteer of a lower social order would take the responsibility on himself, get punished and thus shelter the real culprit, who escaped without the slightest inconvenience to himself. Slaves would voluntarily suffer even capital punishment in place of the man they considered their rightful chief, and the whole country knew, kept silent, and rejoiced at any similar trick played on Bula Matadi, by which name the State authorities were known. This was not caused by any particular dislike for the men who represented the new order of things, it was simply a last stand for the old-established customs by a race that refused to die without kicking.[1]

During the French Revolution a great many instances of the revival of apparently dead customs occurred, and in fact practically every rising of a relatively submissive people in the face of dominant and superior conquerors gives us illustrations of this. Almost exactly the same sort of reversion mechanism marks mental disease in the individual. Strong and important human tendencies, such as those which cluster around the long-established traditions of a group, cannot be forcibly repressed without producing a dangerous state of lack of balance.

If we take the other two cases in which groups meet, neither group being overwhelmingly assertive or submissive, or both groups being friendly, there is always much interchange of custom; but any custom which is assimilated is given a form characteristic of the group which takes it over. The adopted custom has to be fitted into a framework of existing institutions, and will never persist for long exactly as it is taken over. At the same time nobody can exactly foretell what form the new custom will take. All that can be said is that it will be made more and more to approximate to existing traditions. Thus,

[1] *On the Trail of the Bushongo*, London, 1925, 19-20.

as fashions move from group to group throughout a community, each society concerned gives them its own twist, in accord with its own past traditions, and the fashion or custom with a single source may have an infinitely varied expression.

The main secret of building up a strong social group is first to encourage the contact of groups, and second to try to see that the group concerned is neither merely submissive nor merely assertive. For this is the type of social contact which leads to genuine social constructiveness and the growth of stable new social forms.

There are, however, obvious limits to what a group can take over from another. No group can assimilate anything for which there is not already some foundation in its existing institutions. To take a group of private soldiers and to try to force upon them at once many of the features of an English Public School or University code is to court failure. Generally speaking, at all levels of social development anything having an obvious practical use in relation to any of the vital needs of life can be transmitted readily from one group to another. " It is," says Rivers, "the knife and the match, the steamship, the house and its furniture, but above and beyond all the firearms of the European which impress the man of rude culture and lead him to regard their possessors as beings of a higher order than himself."[1] With differences for materials, the same thing is true at all social levels. When we want to bring one group

[1] *Psychology and Ethnology*, London, 1926, 303.

114

into touch with another, by far the best way of doing so is to work through the medium of some custom, or institution, or possession of the one group which the other one has also, but has less effectively.

The question of borrowing, as contrasted with that of contact, brings us face to face with the important problem of the limits of individual initiative in society. The modern world has developed social mechanisms which are definitely intended to stimulate borrowing from one group to another. Thus, for example, every army has its military representatives in foreign friendly countries. Picked men from one branch of a fighting service are definitely given opportunity to observe the training and practices of other branches. Meetings are arranged between representatives of one service and those of another. It is equally easy to find illustration of the same characteristic of modern society from civilian social organisation. All this is a tacit recognition of the fact that social progress is mainly due to influences coming from outside the group that develops.

At the same time it must be recognised that there are the same sort of psychological limits to borrowing as there are to contact. A man trained in one environment and then placed in another will not react equally to all the elements of his new situation. Some of them he will completely ignore ; others will make no lasting impression upon him. Only those in tune with his own predominant instincts and temperamental qualities will seem to him to be worth lifting and transferring to his native group.

Further, *how* the borrowed elements gain a footing in the group of the borrower depends largely upon the latter's peculiar temperament. It very often happens that the most ready and the most broad-minded borrower is of the friendly, persuasive type. This is because a man of that kind easily sympathises with or "understands" others, and it is often highly suggestible. When he returns to his group to attempt to transmit the borrowed elements he must adopt the same persuasive, rather than the assertive, method. Thus the materials borrowed are ready to get whittled down into the shape of already existing group institutions and speedily to lose their peculiar stamp. The situation never is as simple as this, however. For practically the only way in which an element coming from outside is able to make headway in an established group is by the formation of a special set of persons directly around the new element who will try to push it through the rest of the community. Any such group always attracts persons in the established group who possess the radical, nonconforming type of personality. The borrower, being the centre of this group, is directly influenced by it, and the chances are that he begins to emphasise the differences between the old group practices and the changes that he wishes to make. He may very likely appear to be directly antagonistic to the old practices, and may, if the resistance of those outside his group continues, become fanatical and extreme, after the fashion of a large number of reformers. Yet all the time, if the custom which he advocates does make headway, it is being modified by its setting in the established culture and brought nearer and nearer to this, so that in the end it may not seem to contain anything very new after all. It is a good thing to know this general psychological history of social reforms, because then, if at some time we should wish to play the part of the reformer, we shall be prepared for what is most likely to happen.

Finally it is important to notice two general conditions leading to the downfall of groups. The first, paradoxically, is where a special group achieves a position of almost complete dominance in the community to which it belongs. When it does this, the bonds of its relationship to other groups become slack. It grows self-contained, and never imports anything from outside itself. Losing touch with all other groups, it forgets the very secret of social power and advancement, and is sure, sooner or later, to degenerate. This has often been the fate of very strong ceremonial or religious groups. The other condition is, on the face of it, the exact opposite, where the group opens its ranks easily to all-comers. Then it loses its secrets and its special functions. It suffers in prestige and sooner or later it, too, inevitably decays. Broadly speaking, it is true to say that if it is very difficult to get outside a group, or if it is very easy to get inside a group, that group is on the way to decay.

Chapter IV. DISCIPLINE AND PUNISHMENT

FROM a psychological point of view discipline may be defined as *enforced obedience to external authority*. This may seem to be unduly narrow. It includes the case of the man who faces danger steadily because he is afraid of the punishment that may be inflicted upon him if he runs away, but it does not include the case of the man who faces danger willingly because he has formed sentiments of duty, of courage, or of self-respect and from no other compulsion whatever. I make the distinction deliberately, however. Psychologically, discipline goes together with punishment and reward. Wherever there is discipline, the punishment is inflicted by some authority outside the man or the group that is submitted to discipline. Whenever the authority comes from inside the man himself, we get *morale* rather than discipline, though the distinction is less sharp in fact than it may be made in theory.

The need for discipline arises largely from the subordination of individual tendencies to social aims and necessities. "Childhood," says Dr W. H. R. Rivers, "is one long conflict between individual instinctive tendencies and the social traditions and ideals of society."[1] It is, however, easy to make too

[1] *Instinct and the Unconscious*, Cambridge, 1920, 157.

much of this conflict. The real source of discipline is less a clash between individual and society than a struggle between instinctive activities and the control and guidance of such activities in special directions. Even in a solitary individual instincts and appetites may come simultaneously into activity which are not really compatible with one another. A way out of this practical difficulty must be discovered, and whatever way is adopted, some of man's instinctive endowment must be controlled. Further, it should never be forgotten that among man's instinctive make-up some tendencies directly foster social control and do not in any way conflict with it. It is not true, for instance, that the young child is utterly and completely self-centred and self-contained. Very early indeed to develop are friendly and delighted responses to other people. Social groups are by no means merely organisations for correcting and restricting individual behaviour, but have also their positive side of securing individual needs, wishes, and purposes. If it were not so, the authority of society would at all stages be felt as much more harsh and severe than it is.

Thus (1) the necessity for the control of instinctive activity would arise altogether independently of the social group.

(2) Every normal individual possesses, as part of his instinctive endowment, tendencies which lead him to accept social control without question.

(3) Nevertheless discipline always involves control exercised from outside, and many of its most

striking illustrations undoubtedly arise in connexion with a conflict between the individual and society.

The reason for this third fact is a psychological one. Every person's conduct is determined from the beginning not only by tendencies common to himself and all others, but also by tendencies and arrangements of tendencies which are his alone. If we are dealing with instinct or appetite groups, these individual idiosyncrasies practically need not enter into our consideration at all; and as a matter of fact neither discipline nor punishment exists within a purely instinctive or appetite group. But I have already said that at the human level no purely instinctive or appetite group is found. All known human groups are, to some extent, interest groups, organised by institution, custom, and tradition. Institutions, customs, and traditions demand a uniformity of behaviour which may run counter to that part of a man's endowment which expresses his own individual tendencies, and at the same time there is in the interest group, as we have seen, the basis for a growth of appeal and the exercise of public control. Thus, strictly speaking, discipline, in so far as it arises from life in society, is not so much merely the control of instincts as the control of that particular arrangement of instinctive tendencies and innate aptitudes which constitutes a man's peculiar temperament or personality.

There is another reason which makes discipline especially necessary within the group. This is the fact, which we have already discussed, of the very great power of persistence of institutions, customs, and traditions.

Once established, in the type of group with which we are most familiar, the institution tends to become itself the centre of the organisation and to persist long after the facts which led to its establishment may have changed. There are also two general situations in which discipline is obviously of particular importance : the first is the case of all new-comers to a group who have not yet assimilated the group habits, and the second is the case of individuals who are at the same time members of different groups differently organised from the point of view of social structure and function.

We must now consider how discipline may be enforced. The indirect method is by the use of punishment ; the direct method by the establishment of some form of unquestioned prestige. It may be said that there is a third method, by education and reason, but this takes us from discipline to *morale*. I shall deal in this chapter only with the use of punishment.

Punishment, as a means of enforcing discipline, depends upon the psychological fact that one instinctive activity or appetite can control another. Thus a man or animal that is sufficiently hungry can face without flinching a danger from which he would under normal circumstances run away. Similarly pugnacity, once it is violently awakened, can control danger-reactions, and the tendency to sleep can, in circumstances of great fatigue, over-ride all other tendencies.

Such control of one instinct by another is apt to be a violent and rather savage business. The controlled instinct is, in fact, less controlled than temporarily swept completely out of the way. There is no reason to believe that its psychological nature is in any way changed by this. The instinct is merely, for the time being, superseded. Later it may function again unaffected by its temporary deposition.

This method of control itself depends upon just those factors that appetite and instinct themselves depend on, that is to say upon organic or environ-mental factors, and consequently it is very apt to fail in an emergency. Now punishment is undoubtedly in origin based upon the fact that one instinct can hold up, replace, and in a sense control another. Just as the control of one instinct by another is a relatively primitive way of influencing conduct, so enforcement of discipline by punishment is most effective in groups which do not belong to a very high level of social development. Psychologically, punishment is fundamentally an appeal to fear and the group of danger-reactions. It is an attempt to control all conduct by creating a state of affairs in which one overmastering fear or dread sweeps away everything else. In the course of social development it gets more and more refined, graded, and made to "fit the crime"; but this still remains its psycho-logical character.

We can at once see reasons why punishment always is, and psychologically must be, very severe and ungraded in groups at a lowly level of social development. In a rough and uncivilised environment the facing of danger and the endurance of hardship are part of a man's daily task. A fear that is to control all others must thus strike at life itself, or at something without which life is accounted pretty well worthless. So that when there does arise a clash between social institutions and individual behaviour, if the individual is to be controlled by society, the fear that is threatened must be an intense one.

This again is part of the psychological justification for the fact that in war punishment at once tends to become more severe, and irregularities which in peace can be adequately controlled by a lesser threat now demand a greater. For in war the *normal* dangers, fears, and hardships are all greatly increased.

Once any system of punishment is set up in a social group, it tends to be perpetuated, just as every other group custom and institution tends to persist. To replace it immediately or wholly by one based upon a different grading of threat, or by a new way of enforcing discipline, always leads to trouble. This is why, when members of a "higher" civilisation have to control members of a "lower", they often say that the only sort of discipline that the latter can understand is a discipline based upon severe and even savage punishment. The statement is often true, if by "can understand" we mean "do understand".

There is another sort of group which has played a great part in past history, and particularly in past military history, in which discipline appears to demand inordinately severe punishment. This is the mercenary army. It consists of men drawn from the most diverse social and national groups, held together, on the whole, by no single truly internal bond, but by the greed for external reward; and practically the only unitary instinctive control that can be invoked in such cases is the fear of death. Thus the most successful commanders in mercenary armies are nearly always those who rule by rigour and by fear.

The method of controlling one instinct by another, which punishment exploits, looks in some ways as if it ought to be a purely negative one. It prevents certain things from being done, but it does not, by itself, appear to indicate what should be done. This has been seized upon by people who wish to maintain that punishment is never psychologically defensible. As a matter of fact the view is not true. If a man were ever ruled by a single tendency it might be true. But he never is. No individual can in practice be confronted by a mere negative. To say "You must not do this" to a person who has at one and the same time tendencies to do a number of different things obviously means in practice "You must do one of the other things". This is a part of what gives to punishment and fear their great positive value in education. More than this: punishment in real life always has reference to some particular concrete situation. A man is never merely punished. He is punished because, in a certain definite situation, he has adopted a mode of behaviour of which the external authority disapproves. These are not the only things that he might do, however. There are other specific sorts of conduct which the society or other authority over him recognises as established, habitual, or customary things to be done. Punishment then means positively: "You must do *these* things". The trouble about punishment is not that it is negative, but that it provides no means by which a man may be helped to do what the punishment indicates that he must do. It simply assumes that he can do those other things if he likes, and such an assumption is not always quite clearly warranted. Thus punishment may prevent a given tendency from coming into operation, but it does not directly do anything to strengthen another tendency so that this may have a chance to come into operation, and it does not by itself do anything to weaken the undesirable tendency. In these ways its usefulness, even in a relatively primitive group, is somewhat severely restricted.

I must say something about the much disputed question of capital punishment in warfare. Psychology has nothing to do with the moral right or wrong of this, but only with how it works in relation to human character, with its effects upon conduct. I have shown already that in time of war, in a fighting force, the recognised punishment for anti-social conduct inevitably and naturally becomes more severe.[1] This is partly because the fighting group in warfare tends to become a relatively primitive type of group and social standards are consequently maintained by relatively primitive methods; and partly because, in an environment which continually imposes hardship and danger, the kind of fear that can control conduct must be proportionately greater. We also saw how, in any group which is organised in the main by appetite and instinct, when any individual behaves differently from the others, the group is apt to turn upon him and crush him. The psychological reason for this is that such behaviour breaks up the group in a way opposed to its normal dispersion as a result of the satisfaction of the appetite or instinct concerned. Capital punishment for desertion from a fighting group in face of the enemy in warfare is simply a regularised and official form of this, and has exactly the same psychological justification. The difficulty about capital punishment is, not that it is psychologically ineffective or unsound, but that not all cases of desertion can be treated as though they were on a level.[2] A man may desert from conscious and deliberate cowardice or fear of danger. He may

[1] See page 6 of the *Report of the Interdepartmental Committee on Proposed Disciplinary Amendments of the Army and Air Force Acts.* London 1925.
[2] See page 3 of the *Report* cited.

also, under certain circumstances, desert because he genuinely and without conscious purpose forgets who he is, where his unit is, and what he has to do in relation to his unit. In a primitive society the punishment, or reprisal, that is inflicted is un-reflective and immediate. But, as at the level of interest groups everywhere we find institutions arising in connexion with all kinds of special social functions, so punishment comes to be the concern of a special group with its standards of social con-duct. It is a part of the business of such a group in a fighting army to inquire, not merely into the fact of desertion, but into its psychological causation. Put a man with a certain mental make-up into a condition of extreme danger, and he will be about as certain to desert as a man with a strong pre-disposition to catch colds will want a doctor if he is made to live with a group of influenza patients. Desertion from involuntary loss of memory must be distinguished from desertion from cowardice. A psychologist need not quarrel with capital punish-ment in the second case, but he must insist upon thorough investigation in the first. This, of course, means that those officers who are responsible for the conduct of courts-martial should have some knowledge of modern psychology; but the import-ance of such a requirement is sufficiently obvious.

Chapter V. DISCIPLINE AND SUGGESTION

Suggestion as a means of enforcing discipline is much more emphatically positive in practice than is punishment, for it is directed to indicating what should be done rather than what should not be done.

In common conversation the term "suggestion" is often used when one person makes a hint to another and the second at once takes this to mean something more, or something more definite, than has actually been said. In the most striking cases this has reference to action. When we act upon a hint rather than on a definite command we are often said to act by suggestion. In all such cases we act without in any way making clear to ourselves what we are doing or why we are doing it.

Many writers on suggestion emphasise this uncritical attitude on the part of the person who receives the suggestion and make it the leading and most essential part of the whole process. This is somewhat misleading. There are at least three general situations in which suggestion occurs, and it is important to distinguish these one from another. Each is based upon its own appropriate social relationship. First there is the case in which mere hints are accepted, interpreted, and usually acted upon without question or criticism. This is very liable to occur in any coherent social group the various members of which are friendly and companionable one with another. It is the type of suggestion which springs from what I have called "primitive comradeship",[1] and, as I shall show, it may be very important indeed in aiding to maintain discipline.

Second there is the case in which commands which are fully formulated are accepted without a trace of criticism or of consideration of their grounds, and are acted upon. This is the type of suggestion which springs out of a social relation of dominance on the one hand and submissiveness on the other. At least it always involves submissiveness on the one side, although the dominance on the other side may be very much veiled or hardly present at all. Such a form is often termed "prestige suggestion", and its most outstanding and extreme illustrations are to be found in certain cases of hypnotism. The relation of the second to the first type raises some interesting questions which I will discuss later.

In the third place there is undoubtedly a type of suggestion in which what is conveyed is certainly criticised, and adversely criticised, but yet it is accepted. The person who receives the suggestion first opposes it, maybe definitely fights against it, but eventually he accepts and acts upon it, and this without any reasoned evaluation of its grounds. The social relationship underlying this type is an extremely complex one, in which both sides involved are striving for dominance, or in which one at least

[1] *Psychology and Primitive Culture*, Cambridge, 1923, 37 ff.

is only relatively submissive; but nevertheless one side domineers over the other.

The process by which hints, half formulated views, commands merely indicated by swift gesture, or some external happening are interpreted, accepted, and carried out without a trace of criticism or of conscious resistance is evidently one that is deeply built into the nature of the social group. It is, as Dr Rivers has pointed out, a potent means of producing unity or uniformity of social action. Rivers connects suggestion directly with gregariousness and believes that as gregariousness varies greatly in different groups, so, in the same way, the influence of suggestion varies.

The Melanesian [he says] is distinctly more gregarious than the average European. His whole social system is on a communistic basis, and communistic principles work throughout the whole of his society with a harmony which is present only in certain aspects of the activity of our own society, and even there the harmony is less complete than in Melanesia. As an example of such harmony I give the following experience. When in the Solomon Islands in 1908 with Mr A. M. Hocart we spent some time in a schooner visiting different parts of the island of Vella Lavella. Whenever we were going ashore five of the crew would row us in the whale boat, four rowing and the fifth taking the steer-oar. As soon as we announced our intention to go ashore, five of the crew would at once separate from the rest and man the boat; one would go to the steer-oar and the others to the four thwarts. Never once was there any sign of disagreement or doubt which of the ship's company should man the boat, nor was there any hesitation who should take the steer-oar, though, at any rate according to our ideas, the coxswain had a far easier and more interesting task than the rest. It is possible that there was some understanding by which the members of the crew arranged who should undertake the different kinds of work, but we could discover no evidence whatever of any such arrangement. The harmony seems to have been due to such delicacy of social adjustment that the intention of five of the members of the crew to man the boat and of one to take the steer-oar was at once intuited by the rest. Such an explanation of the harmony is in agreement with many other aspects of the social behaviour of Melanesian or other lowly peoples.[1]

Rivers gives numerous further illustrations of the same alleged process. It is possible that some of his facts could be controverted and some of his interpretations questioned, but there seems no reason to doubt that in the nature of society there is something that predisposes the individuals concerned to accept and act upon hints and half-expressed views and commands conveyed through other members of the same group. Thus there is facilitated a unity of thought, feeling, and action which may run throughout a whole community. The more all the individuals in a group are on a level, none being markedly superior and none markedly inferior in their social relationships, the more this is likely to happen. Thus Rivers's groups were not groups with a single outstanding leader. But around the process special social devices soon grow up, and these can be and are consciously and deliberately controlled. I have shown that in the most primitive group a

---

[1] *Instinct and the Unconscious*, 94–5.

leader, when he emerges, does so directly on the basis of the possession of certain personal characteristics. Soon, however, he gives place to the leadership which is established on the basis of an hereditary rank or an official class. Once that step is taken, the capacity of the leader to enforce unitary action or discipline upon his men very soon comes to be bound up with the development of symbols; badges, insignia, special dress of various kinds. These aid him powerfully to maintain order, not because their significance or their reason is thought about at all, but because they constantly hint or suggest to his men that the latter should adopt a certain attitude of acceptance, until direct obedience may have become an established habit.

Another important matter, equally psychological in its foundation, calls for consideration at this point. A period of rest, interposed between periods of fighting, if it is at the same time a period of official inactivity, is often peculiarly demoralising. Then is the time for rigorous and vigorous parade drill. This is useful, not in order to produce more efficiency in certain muscular exercises, and certainly not because these regular and stereotyped evolutions are directly applicable to the fighting which will follow, but because of its suggestive influence in maintaining an attitude of controlled, alert, trained respect for authority without which no body of men will for long hold together and be an effective unit as a fighting group.

Uniforms, insignia of office, traditional ways in

which orders are given, elaborate and stereotyped parades may all be of the greatest importance in indirectly suggesting and fostering an attitude favourable to discipline. At. the same time they, like punishment, remain, for the most part, agents outside the men who are to be dealt with. Within limits, if they are changed, the attitude of unreasoned and unquestioned obedience soon breaks down. They are more positive than punishment, but they, like punishment, do not by themselves genuinely strengthen a man to do what they indicate to him that he is expected to do.

That all these indirect, half-stated, half-hidden ways of inducing and maintaining respect for and obedience to authority should be given their full scope is the more necessary since in war occasions often arise which tend very greatly to heighten suggestibility. For example, Rhode, a German doctor, records how he several times observed the vast increase of suggestibility which followed upon long and tiring marches undertaken during the early stages of the late European war. During a retreat at night, let a single soldier, weary and downcast, throw himself on the side of the road and give way to an attack of "nerves", and in an hour or so a hundred men would be in the same plight.[1] Effects of this sort are, as every soldier knows, exceedingly common. Spreading rapidly by suggestion, they can, by similar but directed subtle working upon the

[1] G. Dumas and H. Aimé, *Névroses et Psychonévroses de Guerre chez les Austro-Allemands*, Paris, 1918, 25.

human mind, be counteracted. An officer who realises the potent influence of this form of suggestion and who keeps calm himself, can often either nip suggestion in the bud, or himself make use of counter-suggestion to avert a threatened crisis.

The second type of suggestion is frequently supposed to apply especially to the proper relationship between an officer and his subordinates. In this type a command is fully formulated and issued. There may be, and usually is, definite dominance on one side, and there is always submissiveness on the other. The command is accepted and acted upon without any criticism or any witting resistance. It is sometimes urged that this attitude of unreasoned acceptance of authority is the attitude which, above any other, should be fostered in the ordinary private soldier. But any discipline which is based wholly or mainly on this is in a very precarious position indeed, as a little psychological analysis will show.

In the first type of suggestion we have considered, the person who receives the hints is able to supply his own interpretation of them because he and whoever conveys the hints display a unity of ways of thinking, feeling, and acting which is the basis of their social comradeship. In this second type, the command being fully and definitely formulated, the subordinate does not himself provide the interpretation, but is to be forced to accept it. There are obvious psychological limits to what can be accepted in this way. A simple illustration will make the difficulty clear.

Suppose a man to be taking a long railway-journey. Opposite to him in the carriage, and staring at him from the fields through which the train passes, is the peremptory advertisement "Buy Blogg's Pen." He sees this, but takes no particular notice of it. At his journey's end he wishes to send off a post-card to tell of his safe arrival. He then finds that he has forgotten or lost his pen. He turns into the first stationer's shop he comes to and, without thinking at all, at once asks "Have you a Blogg's pen?"

This may be treated as an instance of uncritical action upon a fully formulated suggestion. But the efficacy of the suggestion obviously depends upon the man's actually needing the pen at a given moment. If his own pen had not been lost or forgotten, or if he had not wished to write, the suggestive advertisement would not have been acted upon so far as this man was concerned. Thus fully formulated suggestions are acted upon without criticism only when they chime in with tendencies in the actor which are awake and ready to burst into action. Suggestion by submissiveness, as we may call it, is bound to break down if the command conveyed runs counter to the fundamental tendencies of the person to whom it is given.

If discipline is to be maintained through the help of this sort of suggestion, the necessary training can never stop short at inducing a submissive attitude in subordinates. Far more important is it to foster the tendencies by means of which alone the commands of the superior can be carried out. Thus in the course of developing the conditions which render the second type of suggestion effective groups may be formed within which the first type becomes possible.

The third type of suggestion, in which opposition is overborne, thrust aside, and rendered of no account by the masterfulness of the superior has very little relationship to any healthy state of collective discipline. Consequently, although its undoubted occurrence raises some attractive psychological problems, I do not propose to discuss it here. Even as a relationship between individuals it is liable to great disturbances, and as a rule imposes a heavy strain on both parties concerned. Very few leaders indeed are capable of dealing in this way with whole groups for long, and none but the definitely domineering kind of leader ought ever to try.

This general discussion may be closed by a very few remarks about the relation of reward to discipline. Reward may in fact be regarded as a type of indirect suggestion, and is also positive in its emphasis. There is only one way in which rewards are of genuine psychological significance in the promotion of any desired end. This is to make the reward such that it itself carries further the very process for which it was given. Money, good conduct medals, and all external badges are, apart from the building up around them of sentiments which embrace the very conduct for which they are awarded, psychologically useless. But promotion is not. For promotion is not only a sign that a man has behaved in a disciplined manner, but itself implies that such conduct must be continued and even improved upon. If promotion does not mean that, it has no psychological efficiency in promoting discipline.

At this point, perhaps, it might seem as if I ought to discuss the characteristics of the good disciplinarian. I propose to do this, however, in connection with a study of leaders and leadership which will form the subject-matter of the next chapter.

Chapter VI. LEADERS AND LEADERSHIP

EVERYBODY agrees that a good leader must take trouble to know the character and capacity of his rank and file, and this is undoubtedly true. It is equally important that a leader should take trouble to know his own character and capacity, and understand clearly what it is that maintains his own authority over his men. From this point, therefore, I propose to begin a brief study of leaders and leadership.

We need not discuss whether the simplest groups must have leaders or not. Some writers think that the earliest kind of social groups are leaderless, others that they are essentially a number of people ranged around a despotic leader. The groups with which we are concerned, in any case, all possess a firmly established and finely graded system of official leadership. They are already at the stage at which leadership as an institution is able to take over some of the functions and authority of the leader as a person.

Broadly speaking, sectional leaders in a complex modern social organisation such as an army may be grouped into three classes :

(*a*) the men who maintain their position mainly by virtue of the established social prestige attaching to their office ;

(*b*) the men who maintain their position mainly

by virtue of their personal capacity to impress and dominate their followers, and

(*c*) the men who maintain their position mainly by virtue of their personal capacity to express and persuade their followers.

I propose to call the first the *institutional* type, the second the *dominant* type and the third the *persuasive* type.

It is often supposed that a leader makes his own position, and by the force of his own character pushes himself to the front. In point of fact, which type of leader comes uppermost at any time depends far more upon the relationship of the group concerned to other groups than upon any other factor. Wherever there is a complex group, possessing an established culture, living under settled and peaceful conditions and relatively self-contained, the institutional type of leader abounds, as, for instance, in an army in peace-time and in most sections of the modern Church, except when theological discussion becomes violent. Whenever antagonisms arise between group and group and become bitter to the point of fighting, the dominant leader has his best chance. Whenever there is much bargaining to be done between group and group and disagreement stimulates discussion, the persuasive leader plays his part : the persuasive is, in fact, the political, the civil, the administrative type of leadership.

I shall take in turn these three types of leader and consider some of their outstanding characteristics.

Originally social groups are organised directly by instinctive and appetitive impulses. The leaders who come to the front do so because they possess in a marked degree the very drive which holds the group together. The fighter, the glutton, the man of inordinate vanity and so on—each has his great chance in a specific sort of appetite group. But before long customs and institutions and the sentiments that cluster around them tend to replace instinct and appetite as the organising agencies of society. Then the acknowledged leader may act really as a symbol of an institution, and not primarily by virtue of personal force or craft. If he does, the secret of his success depends mainly upon his doing nothing to disturb the social sentiments that are attached to certain established institutions of his group. Sentiments are always turned chiefly towards the past, and the social sentiments form no exception to this rule. They rest upon persisting factors in group organisation. They help to stabilise all kinds of devices—uniforms, hidden formulae, catch-words, badges, flags, symbols of all sorts—for maintaining the past. The institutional leader is and must be punctilious about these things, conservative about them. If he lets them slip, his authority has gone. He must learn how they were acquired and what they are regarded as standing for, and he must attach his followers to *them* rather than to himself, so that an affront to them will be resisted and a change in them resented. Such a leader may maintain authority and build up a thoroughly coherent group. The danger with this group is that it inevitably tends to become rather narrowly self-contained and non-adaptable. If by force of circumstances it is thrown into close contact with groups of another type, it may show itself rigid and unfriendly. Nevertheless this is the only way in which the leader whose power is in his post rather than in himself can consolidate his authority. He may be fussy and punctilious to the last degree about details of dress, drill, and formal discipline. Others are certain to laugh at him for his rigidity and love of past times. But he is right psychologically, and if a man goes to a position of leadership who lacks the personal qualities either to dominate or to understand his men, he may yet make a very considerable success provided he frankly recognises this and suits his method to his character.

Perhaps it goes without saying that there are many more men of this type than of any other. Such a leader, since he must emphasise rank, has to maintain an attitude of aloofness in general so far as his followers are concerned. We commonly say that a leader is born and not made, but leaders of this type can be, and are, most admirably turned out to pattern to the tune of hundreds a year, in the appropriate training colleges.

The dominant type of leader, who impresses, commands, shapes, and sways his men, presents us with extremely interesting psychological problems. I think it certain that the innate basis of this type of character is so important and strong that nobody who does not possess it can by training learn to control men in the dominant manner. It is in reference to the second and third class of leaders that it is more or less true to say that a leader is born and not made.

The dominant leader draws his power directly from the strength in him of the social instinct of assertiveness. But it is clear enough that this alone will not take him far. Plenty of people who are constantly making strenuous efforts to assert themselves are by no means successful leaders, and probably no successful leadership ever was based upon this alone.

This type of leader possesses a capacity for swift decision. When others are still thinking about a thing or hesitating over an action, he has reached his conclusion or is already in action. The institutional leader will base his decision on precedent, and must know what others have done before him. This is not necessary for the dominant leader, although it may often be a good thing in him. He can outrage precedent and still retain his power over his men, for they are attached to him rather than to the institution. His temperament is ardent, his intellectual and emotional processes are quick, and though they need not be profound, of course they often are.

In actual life the dominant leader is nearly always found in a type of group that is chiefly concerned with action; or if with thought, then with a type of thinking which exalts the importance of activity.

Thus he is commonly very much of a practical turn of mind and can readily leap the gap between ideas, or feelings, and actions. He generally has the reputation of being perfectly willing to do what he orders his men to do, and the reputation is generally deserved.

As a rule the dominant leader is not merely the type of man who takes responsibility when it is given to him; he definitely goes out to look for it. That is what gives him much of his hold over men; for the ordinary man is rarely anxious to shoulder more responsibility than the normal course of life in society thrusts upon him, and if anybody is willing to take responsibility from him he will usually obey such a man.

The dominant leader is never much afraid of making mistakes. He knows that his power resides not in what he does but in himself. From the point of view of the outside critic he will often blunder, and within limits blunder badly, but his power over those whom he actually meets does not suffer by that. Consequently on this count also he is far more able than the institutional leader to initiate new movements and to bring about radical changes in his group.

There is a type of dominant leader who remains rather cold and aloof from his men. We usually call him domineering. We may resent what he does, but all the same we submit to it. There is another type who can mix with his men on terms of apparent equality and yet lose none of his power. In this respect again the dominant type differs from the institutional type. For the latter, as we have seen, tends to lose his authority if he does not remain somewhat self-contained and keep his distance from his followers. But the dominant leader can laugh with a man as if he were merely a fellow-being at one moment, and freeze him with an order at the next. Napoleon could do this, as everybody knows, and perhaps it is hardly too much to say that all genuinely great war captains down to those of the last great war of all were men of the dominant type.

All leadership, however, is of the nature of an interplay between the group led and the leader or the institution of leadership. This is true even when the leader is of the dominant type, for rarely, perhaps never, is a man equally dominant in all kinds of groups. In fact what we usually see is that a man, dominant in one group, on going to another one is altogether incapable of taking the lead. For example, a man may be truculently dominant in his own circumscribed political group and in his own constituency, but in the House of Commons he subsides into impotence. If local prophets spoke truly, the British Cabinet would speedily become much larger even than it is.

These considerations raise the very interesting question of how far dominance in a leader depends upon specialised efficiency or skill. The truth about this is that special efficiency and technical knowledge may help a leader to maintain his position, but will not give him dominance, except—and even this is doubtful—in a very special kind of group. Perhaps we can go further than this, and say that in many groups a dominant personality nevertheless will not and cannot achieve the rank of leader unless at the same time he possesses specialised skill or knowledge. The primary bases of great skill and of great intelligence are no doubt innate, just as much as is that peculiar blend of decisiveness, capacity for action, assertiveness, and power to arouse respect which constitutes dominance. But obviously a great amount of skill and knowledge must be acquired. So that although a dominant leader can within limits neglect precedents and pay scanty attention to history, it may still be highly necessary for him to pay close and careful attention to contemporary ways of doing things and to contemporary knowledge. How far this is true depends upon his group rather than upon himself, and particularly upon the relationship of his group to other groups. The palmy days of the dominant leader are the days in which groups have relatively unspecialised social functions, and those in which different groups come into definite antagonism. It has repeatedly been shown that development, whether we take society in general or whether we take a special group such as an army, proceeds more and more towards complexity of social structure with consequent increased specialisation of groups. Many of these specialisations depend directly upon technical advances in skill and knowledge, and consequently the general drift of social development is away from the despotic and dominant type of leader towards the institutional or persuasive type. Where the dominant type is still found, he often has to maintain his authority by special skill or by special knowledge, although he may have gained his authority by personal characteristics with which special skill and knowledge have practically nothing to do. But as soon as antagonistic group relationships are set up there is a tendency for the dominance based directly upon personal character to come to the front again.

A leader who knows that his ascendancy over his followers is based upon his personal power to command and impress people has two things which he must constantly consider. The first is how far the group which he leads is specialised either for skill or for knowledge, and the second is what is the nature of the inter-relations between his group and others. Broadly, the less specialised the functions of the group and the more antagonistic its relations to other groups, the more he can rely directly upon his personal character and the less does he need to rest upon acquired skill and knowledge. Conversely, the more specialised the group and the more friendly its relationships to other groups, the more he must rely upon training himself, or being trained, in skill and knowledge. To this extent training enters largely into the production of a good leader, even of the dominant type, in the modern world.

The persuasive type of leader is in many respects psychologically the most interesting of all. He is as a rule very much the most complex and subtle character. We commonly picture the position of a chief to his followers in a relatively primitive group as due directly to his dominance or assertiveness. But many records suggest that this is far from being true. Other qualities than these may recommend him to his fellows, and comparatively early there may grow up a leadership which "does not depend mainly upon domination or assertion, but upon a ready susceptibility to the thoughts, feelings, and actions of the members of the group. The chief, that is, *expresses* the group rather than *impresses* it".[1] This type of leadership tends to play a greater and greater part as social life develops. It is, as I have said, the civil type, the administrative type. It is particularly in place in a tolerably settled community within which there are a number of groups in close contact and friendly relationship, and with much negotiation to be carried on between them.

We have all met this type of leader. He has extraordinary capacity for knowing what people are thinking about, or feeling, or doing, and of divining what they are going to think, feel, or do next. This is based, I think, upon a very high degree of suggestibility, upon a capacity to react to hints which are not yet formulated and which more ordinary people fail to respond to altogether. We speak of him as "understanding" men. He announces a policy and everybody thinks: "Oh yes, that was exactly what we wanted. In fact we were all going

[1] *Psychology and Primitive Culture*, 79.

to say the same thing, only he is so clever that he always 'gets there' first". He has, as a rule, a great capacity for formulation. He loves making speeches and is good at the job. His group may provide him with ideas, but he finds the words and then everybody thinks that he has also discovered the ideas. He need not be the active, emotional type, but he is the alert intellectual type. He excels in assimilation. He is apt to be inconsistent, but no more so than the group he leads, and thus both he and his followers may be perfectly honest in formulating and acting upon contradictories. There is perhaps only one thing that this leader can never afford to do, and that is to get out of touch with his group. If he does, his power has gone. The institutional leader *must* remain aloof; the dominant leader *may* remain aloof; the persuasive leader *dare not* remain aloof. Thus if his group grows large, he has to have a kind of secret service about him, and the dangers of that hardly need comment.

The persuasive type of leader nearly always comes to the top whenever different fairly friendly groups have to negotiate with one another for any purpose, and is, for the same sort of reason, useful in administration. The institutional leader is very often particularly hopeless outside of his own special group and the same may be true, to a lesser degree perhaps, of the dominant leader. But the persuasive leader, reacting as he does to the hints, desires, wishes, half-formulated ambitions and tendencies of men, can be almost equally at home in groups which in social structure and functions are very different. He can thus discover common bases for agreement, and his most frequent method of dealing with any kind of social problem is by compromise.

Obviously this ready impressionability may be greatly facilitated by direct acquaintance with specialised skill or technical knowledge. It never depends upon that, however. In particular it does not depend to any important extent upon the actual possession by the leader of either a high degree of technical skill or of detailed knowledge. It is more true of the persuasive type of leader than of any other that he is born and not made. But no doubt it is also true that he improves his power of interpretation by exercising it.

All these remarks bear directly upon the practical question of the choice of leaders. It is possible to make a few general statements about this which hold true in the majority of cases.

Where a leader is of the institutional type, it is always far better that he should be chosen from a social class or rank different from that of the majority of his followers. Then both he and his position will suffer least from that aloofness which his character imposes upon him.

Where a leader has to be chosen from the same social class or rank, he should be of the dominant or the persuasive type according to the kind of group that he has to control.

On the whole, self-contained groups in a fairly settled community favour the institutional type of leader. Self-contained groups in a community under-going rapid change, and especially where different groups are antagonistic, favour the dominant type of leader. Groups in a relatively settled community which are in pretty close and friendly contact, or have to enter into bargaining and negotiation one with another, directly favour the persuasive type of leader.

It goes without saying that types are not indi-viduals, and that few leaders of society whom we actually meet will fit completely into any of the frames which I have constructed in this chapter. In particular, the enormous complexity of present social grouping and its capacity for increasing antagonisms between group and group to a point of great bitterness with little or no actual physical violence produces a considerable crop of leaders who are a blend of the persuasive and the dominant. These are apt to possess the ready vocabulary and the linguistic fluency of the first, together with the relative lack of adaptability of the second. This is one of the several reasons for the devastating power of the "slogan" in most forms of civilised social competition.

Finally, we return to the question of the charac-teristics of the good disciplinarian. It should now be clear that there is no single best method by which he does his work. He varies his method to suit his group and in consonance with his own personality. But one thing is always true of him, and that is that he is never much worried about questions of abstract justice. His problems are practical problems and he sees them concretely. A difficulty occurs, he issues his verdict, and then goes on to the next difficulty. The verdict could probably be shown to involve injustice to somebody or other. What of that? All practical verdicts can be shown to involve a measure of injustice. A man who is much concerned with questions of justice to everybody is in practice inevitably vacillating and timid, unless perhaps he is passing a verdict after the event, when he is in a very different position from that of the man who has to decide what the event shall be. He may be a sharp critic, but he is a poor executor. In a world of clashing interests and tendencies, of unequal intelligences, and of infinitely varied sensibilities, the man who is always troubled by a desire to "do right by everybody" is in a very miserable state. This is what often earns the good disciplinarian an unmerited reputation for lack of sympathy. Once his decision is taken, he usually treats the particular affair that demanded his intervention as closed so far as he is concerned. Only if he has this capacity can he retain the respect of his followers and, for himself, maintain authority without an intolerable strain.

Chapter VII. MORALE, WITH SPECIAL REFERENCE TO GROUP GAMES

*M*ORALE may be defined as : Obedience to authority under external circumstances which impose great strain, the source of authority being within the man, or the group, that is obedient.

Morale produces a steadier, more persistent, less fluctuating type of conduct than discipline. Discipline may break down when punishment is relaxed ; when a leader is killed, or dies, or is defeated; when uniforms are disgraced or removed, flags captured, and the external symptoms of authority degraded. *Morale* depends on none of these things, and so may continue when all external sources of command have broken down. The main secret of a thoroughly sound man, of a cohesive and powerful group, depends upon the development of *morale*. How then can *morale* be developed?

When *The Times* correspondent charged one of the packs in a recent international Rugby football match with lack of discipline, he remarked : "This quality, in strenuous affairs like war and Rugby football, means well-harnessed intelligence and restraint".[1] He was, in effect, urging that *morale* consists in the control of conduct by intelligence. To a considerable extent, and using the word "intelligence" in a wide sense, this is true. I shall,

[1] *The Times*, Jan. 18, 1926.

therefore, attempt to show how such control can be, or at least very often is, developed.

Broadly speaking, there are five stages in the growth of genuine *morale*. These are, of course, given very varying degrees of emphasis in different individual cases, but on the whole they represent with sufficient accuracy the natural history of the growth of *morale*.

The first is the negative stage, as when, for example, a child learns that there are certain things that he must not do. This shows the very important part which may be played by discipline, and often by definite punishment and fear, in the development of *morale*. I have already shown that, human nature being what it is, no person can ever be confronted by a mere negative. To say to a child "You must not do this" always in practice means : "You must do something else". The emphasis is negative, however, and the method of enforcement is, at this stage, mainly external and particularly through some form of punishment. Moreover this negative kind of command is apt to be very restricted in its application. It is easily interpreted to mean : "I must not do this so long as so-and-so is watching" ; or : "I must not do this so long as it is pretty certain that I shall suffer because I shall be found out and be punished by somebody". Again the negative stage usually means : "I must not do this particular thing, or that particular thing, or the other particular thing". So whenever a series of prohibitions tends to solidify into a code of laws, we nearly always get long lists of particular things that must not be done—as in the old Jewish commandments—with no clearly stated or realised connexion between the different things. Such codes can easily become group conventions and may regulate conduct inside the group to which they belong. But once a man gets outside of his group, they may cease to have any binding force upon him, even as negative commands. Thus the negative rules, which seem to be necessary steps in the passage to true *morale*, are apt to be specialised to particular circumstances, people, and groups. Change the circumstances and the rules break down.

Nevertheless when the negative laws are codified into some sort of a system, we are already at the second stage; for, although the connexion between one negative rule and another is not generally stated, we are on the way to a recognition that such a connexion does exist. To form rules into a code is itself a great step towards replacing mere discipline by genuine *morale*.

The third stage, seen very clearly in the growing child, is the extraordinarily important stage of hero-worship. This is a stage which practically all normal children pass through, and probably the best men and women never quite get beyond it. I need not now try to analyse the psychological factors underlying hero-worship. It is enough to say that most men who are not too sophisticated, or too anti-social, or too "superior" possess heroes, and that the moment a hero emerges, conduct ceases to become a mere matter of avoiding things, and becomes positively doing the sort of things that the hero does, or the kind of things that he would approve. One of the most significant services which a dominant leader ever renders to his group is to provide its members with a hero.

Hero-worship is tremendously important psychologically for two reasons. It places the emphasis in conduct upon what should be done, and it provides, not an isolated rule for a particular circumstance, but a system of rules, or, better, a system of conduct. Since the hero is a person and so has many sides, the effort which he stimulates is clearly not simply to do one kind of thing, but to do a lot of things which, put together, make up his mode of life.

Hero-worship, however, is also subject to severe limitations. The hero may die, may change, may fail, may pass out of the life of his worshipper in various ways, and so the mode of living which he has stimulated may be only very temporary.

Again some trivial accident or eccentricity of his may be copied and may be treated as a symbol of the conduct upon which it is really nothing but an excrescence. George Fox, the Quaker, thought that one man was as good as another. Consequently, when he went to see Oliver Cromwell he kept his hat on his head. This seemed an excellent plan to many of his followers, and they easily copied the trivial custom, missing what lay more deeply beneath. So the student copies the tricks of speech and mannerisms of his teacher, and thinks that in this way he acquires the other's profundity of thought. To such vagaries hero-worship is very liable.

Finally, we may, and constantly do, outstrip our heroes and have to find another sanction for conduct. Thus hero-worship does not give us a basis of behaviour which is beyond the tricks of a fleeting fortune. It undoubtedly may be made to play a very important part in the development of *morale* within any active and practical group, such as a company of men who are being trained for war, but it is a step towards the goal rather than itself a means of attaining the goal.

The characteristics of the next stage can best be understood by a study of the influence of games upon the formation of character. I shall make no attempt to discuss in detail the many theories as to the psychological basis of play. According to some writers play is merely the exercise of that superfluous activity which any healthy and vigorous organism possesses. This clearly does not explain why such activity should issue in play rather than in any other direction of effort. Others again treat play as a kind of recapitulation of the history of the race. Thus when the Boy Scout practises camping and raising war-whoops and the like, he is said to be back at a relatively primitive phase of mental and social development. The fact that most games have a competitive element is, according to this theory, to be treated as a civilised way of going to war. The trouble about this is that there is little reason

for believing that primitive people played much
less than we do, or in very different ways—
making due allowance for the differences of environment—from our own.

A third theory treats play from a very different
point of view, as a preparation for more serious
modes of life. There is, of course, no need to assume that people play because they consciously
want to prepare themselves for something else.
Indeed many people do not want to do this. If a
man stops short at play, so that it does not prepare
him for anything beyond itself, his play does not
cease to be play on that account or change its
psychological nature. Still, undoubtedly games can
be used to build up codes of conduct which are
realised as applying far beyond the limits of the
sports field. Let us consider how this is done.

First of all a game is a *positive* kind of effort, for
the most part. Nobody is ever really first-rate at a
game by merely avoiding things that need not be
done. All games in fact assume that there are certain
things that the players want to do, and the emphasis
has to be laid on these.

Secondly, most games played by human beings,
except those played by very young children and by
old gentlemen, tend to be group games. The importance of this, from our point of view, is not
merely that a lot of persons take part in them, but
is much more that they demand co-operation and
combination. There are comparatively few such
games in which each member of a group is doing

the same thing as all the others. Thus it is never merely a question of doing certain things well, but of doing the right thing at the right time. This often means holding a tendency to act in check till the signal is given by some other person, or definitely attempting to modify one way of carrying out an action to fit in with some other way adopted by a different person. This again means the recognition that there may be a variety of ways of getting to the same end. To realise this would appear to be a very simple matter, but many people fail exactly in this respect. The necessity for fitting in with the others in a group game helps to direct attention upon the end of the game rather than exclusively upon any one means of reaching that end. This again helps to lay stress upon the general conduct of the game rather than merely upon special technical skill in detail. Thus we say that, no matter how particular movements in a game are carried out, the individual must play unselfishly, must subordinate his personal aggrandisement to the good of his side, must fit in with others, must control immediate impulses and so on. All of these things, together with a great amount that cannot be formulated in any way, make up the "spirit" of the game, which is independent of particular players, and special occasions. Very few players, of course, trouble to work out all this, or any considerable part of it, for themselves, and it is not in the least necessary that they should do so. The important point is that these things which are here formulated and set out in black and white are, in the game, effective, whether with or without formulation.

In the third place, and probably more important still in the building up of military *morale*, is the fact that practically all forms of game that need be considered are competitive. It is not alone the competition that counts, but more still the fact that the competition is usually carried on at a high speed, and success depends upon a man's retaining at the same time special skill. Direct appeal is made to the instincts of pugnacity and assertiveness, to individual pride and the like. Skill, on the other hand, depends upon intellectual factors to a large extent. Even where it is innate in its basis, in order for a man to exercise skill in the swiftly changing emergences of a competitive game fought out at a rapid pace, he must keep wide awake to all the changes that are going on and must fit his skill to the circumstances. For genuine skill in games is very little a matter of habit, since it has constantly to be adapted to combinations of circumstances which may never have occurred before and may never occur again. Thus the instinctive basis—pugnacity, or whatever it may be—and the acquired skill and its intelligent application have to be united. Probably in no other activities of modern life is this combination so necessary or so important as in vigorous group games and in war; and that is a great part, though not all, of the reason why the first are a good training for the second.

Fourthly, all games and every sport that are of

much use in the establishment of *morale* contain some element of risk, and of resistance to pain. The risk and the pain, however, are so bound up with activities that are genuinely interesting and pleasurable that they lose their terrors and may, in fact, add to the attractiveness of the whole activity. Games and sport help greatly in bringing about that union of reaction to danger and of curiosity and interest in a presented situation which constitutes adventurousness. The positive appreciation of risk and a certain relish for adventure are indispensable parts of *morale* in military life.

In the fifth place, vigorous group games contribute probably more than anything else to the building up of an attitude which is able to see an element of humour in the most dismal circumstances of life. The game may be for the time as serious as real life, but with some of the acerbity of real life softened. Thus if disasters happen, the players learn not merely to bear them, but to "grin and bear them". A capacity to see the funny side of depressing circumstances is a most persistent and characteristic feature at any rate of British *morale*, and I believe of nearly all genuinely gallant behaviour in the face of long-continued trouble. It displays a humour utterly different from levity, and free from bitterness. Again and again this attitude has helped the British soldier through depressing days. The fact that a most dismal dug-out, for instance, should bear the name of some highly luxurious hotel actually helps its inhabitants to laugh their way through considerable misery. I am convinced that the humour with which any ordinary crowd òf British citizens constantly meets circumstances of great difficulty, delicacy and danger, a humour which crops out in every British army in time of war and during almost all civil and political struggles in England, is developed more by the British love of vigorous games than in any other way. It represents perhaps the happiest of all the striking contributions made by group games to the promotion of sound *morale*.

Yet, though all this may be perfectly true, games may fail to build up any genuine *morale*. A man may be—and I am afraid he often is—whatever is meant by a "sportsman" while he is playing a game, and at the same time rather a "rotter" in his other activities in life. The motto "Play the game" has to be extended beyond the game if it is to lead to true *morale*. There is a peculiar, innate, and strong tendency in all human activities to become tied to particular circumstances. The game in which *morale* has to be displayed, however, is the game of life itself, and the very essence of *morale*, as contrasted with mere convention, is that it is not tied to special groups and special circumstances.

Now whenever a man who has discovered that a certain principle holds good in one case extends that principle to another case which is different in some of its details, that man is, in so far as the principle is formulated, using his intelligence. I may run away from danger a hundred times, every case being different in some respects from the rest, and yet may act purely from instinct. But supposing I get interested in these hundred cases and, disregarding their differences, discover that "Every time a situation is held to possess danger a man naturally runs away," my intelligence has been at work. Having arrived at such a principle does not in itself make it any the less likely that I shall continue to run away, and it does not make the running away any the less instinctive; but at least to some extent I am now forearmed.

As a matter of actual fact, intelligence is never likely to be exercised except in cases where some clash of tendencies to action is found. A man has a tendency to run away, but at the same time he has a tendency to stand up and, within limits, to meet whatever comes. It is this sort of practical difficulty that makes him think. In other words, a man thinks only when he is faced with genuine alternatives. Whenever he does think, however, his mental processes follow the same general path. He attempts to analyse the situation he has to deal with, to see how it is built up, and to discover some solution of the difficulties which can be formulated in such a way that it will apply to other similar cases. Thus all rules, whether in games, or in mere intellectual exercises, or in the most serious affairs of life, are the products of thinking. But it hardly needs saying that to form a rule and to learn a rule are not to put it into practice. There is no ideal, no genuine *morale*, without the exercise of intelligence and equally there is no case in which the mere exercise of intelligence itself forms the ideal or completes the *morale*.

There is a curious recent American movement called "The Children's Morality Code"[1]. It offers a code containing eleven laws, each with a number of articles, which small Americans in elementary schools are to be taught to repeat. The code begins with The Law of Self-Control and ends with The Law of Loyalty. It runs thus:

The Law of Self Control.

Good Americans control themselves.

Those who best control themselves can best serve their country.

1. I will control my tongue, and will not allow it to speak mean, vulgar or profane words. I will think before I speak. I will tell the truth and nothing but the truth.

2. I will control my temper, and will not get angry when people or things displease me. Even when indignant against wrong and contradicting falsehood I will keep my self-control.

The code goes on in a similar strain throughout the whole of the eleven laws and all their many articles. The statements made are practically all wholly unexceptionable and err only on the side of perfection. But it is not easy to see exactly what their recitation is expected to do. The better part of every ideal and of all *morale* is a part that cannot be formulated at all.

In the ordinary course of life, as we have repeatedly seen, ways of feeling and acting tend to

[1] By William J. Hutchins, Washington, D.C. 1926.

get organised into stable groups and make what are technically called sentiments. These are very apt to get specially attached to certain groups and certain institutions only, and to have no binding influence upon conduct beyond those groups and institutions. Ways of thinking about things get organised too, and, as always, tend to run beyond the special circumstances which may have stimulated them. Thus, so far as they have to do with conduct, they issue in rules and principles which are much less bound up with particular groups and particular circumstances than is the case with the sentiments. Society has, however, developed ways for keeping these generalised principles of conduct in touch with the sentiments, although the essence of the latter, being mainly concerned with ways of feeling and acting, can hardly be formulated in words at all. The most important of the ways adopted is by the formation of groups in which a demand is made upon the very instincts, and their control and synthesis, which have to be used in the most serious concerns of mature life, but in which the control is the easier because the issue is not a matter of life and death, or anywhere near that. The whole process is made the more certain by having many such groups with an overlapping membership. Beyond doubt the most important groups are those that affect people at an early stage of life. The chief of these are the family; to a far greater extent probably, in many cases, the school or the University; and particularly games groups.

The sensible family or school is not a mere shelter from the outside world, as many people now seem to want to make them, but is the outside world in little, with much of its roughness and cruelty toned down though not entirely removed, and with interests suited to the ages of most of its members. I have already shown that the peculiar value of games is that they reduplicate the issues of serious life, but remove some of their sharpness and finality. What helps to make the family tradition, the school loyalty, the game's unwritten code go far beyond the limits of the group within which they are first practised is that other similar groups have the same sort of code, and that in many instances there is an overlapping membership which makes it very easy to compare codes, and to realise that the practices encouraged in one group have an application which is independent of the group itself.

It is, then, possible to draw certain practical conclusions from this rather theoretical discussion. The formation of *morale* depends mainly on this : first a group must be formed the activities of which call upon those instincts and interests which are the basis of a man's conduct in the most serious affairs of his life. This group will speedily establish recognised and regular ways of carrying out such activities, and around these sentiments will be formed. The activities must be varied so that the instincts and interests which they stimulate have to be controlled by careful adjustment to the demands of the immediate situation. This gives conduct which is a blend of intelligence, feeling, and interest. The next step is to detach this conduct from any specific group badge or group leader. Such a step is greatly facilitated by bringing groups together who have pretty much the same code although they have to deal with different practical problems, or who have different codes although they deal with the same spheres of practical life. It can then be seen that the code need not be merely the product of any particular man, badge, or group, but may have universal application within the general sphere of life concerned. When that is realised, and at the same time the code is not merely intellectually appreciated but used as an organised way of life, it has become an ideal, and as such goes to establish a sound and lasting *morale*.

Of course this is not the whole story. Group ideals may be formed and carried out, but if any of the individual members of the group are for some reason mentally or physically unstable, the *morale* is apt to disappear in moments of high strain. Now, therefore, we have reached the point at which we must go on to discuss mental disease, particularly as it may occur in warfare.

PART THREE

MENTAL HEALTH AND DISEASE IN WARFARE

Chapter I. THE GENERAL BACKGROUND

THROUGHOUT this book I have followed most modern psychologists in regarding all human conduct as based upon, and the expression of, appetites, instincts, and original and acquired interests. We have seen how these all tend to become more specialised and controlled as social and individual life develops. Upon a basis of curiosity grow up all kinds of special technical skill demanding control by carefully acquired knowledge. The growth of group life, and the fitting in of one person with another, constantly demand that individual tendencies should be held in check and controlled by group aims, by the sentiments which are attached to institutions, by the assertive intelligence of the leader and the like. Any lack of balance between competing tendencies for control in the individual is liable to produce a state of mental stress which may very easily become genuine mental disease. Thus the secret of mental health in the individual is very much the same as that of social stability in the group, and its study can perhaps be best approached by considering briefly three common types of social organisation.

First we may consider a group the various individuals of which are almost entirely dominated by one highly active leader. He thinks for the rest, makes them behave as he pleases, and rules over them despotically. Such a group may appear from without to be thoroughly cohesive, efficient, and well knit together. But suppose the leader encounters some problem that is too difficult for him, or suppose he is destroyed, or his power is shattered in any way. At once the group tends to drift apart; it becomes weak and inefficient, and may split up into its individual constituents, who outside the group are nothing like the men they are inside it.

Some men are exactly like that. Their character is made up by the organisation together of all sorts of tendencies to act, feel, and think, some of which are very deep-seated and instinctive, and some acquired in the course of personal experience. Among all these tendencies one, or one group, has won the upper hand completely, and so rules the rest that the man's life entirely centres on the one activity—it may be interest in business, in art, in science, or in sport; it may be love of some person, or attachment to some dogma, or pursuit of some aim such as the prohibition of alcohol, or perpetual motion. The man becomes a fanatic. All is well up to a point. Then age, or change of health, or force of circumstances, or, it may be, success deposes the leading tendency temporarily or permanently, and the man breaks up, "goes to pieces" we say. It is a common thing, for instance, for a man whose business has become the all-absorbing pursuit of his life to appear alert and efficient until he retires. But he has never trained anything else to take the lead. He retires, seeks rest, "moons about," is unhappy, discontented, may even, perhaps die earlier than he need have done, all because his one leading interest has been deposed. This sort of mental breakdown is not uncommon as a result of the setting up of war conditions.

There is another kind of group which also presents a fairly compact, cohesive appearance from the outside, but is all the time divided into factions, cliques, and discordant sects. Here there is divided authority, with no one faction strong enough to control the rest and the various parties out of sympathy one with another. This sort of group may persist successfully until some special emergency arises. Then the divisions become acute. No one faction can maintain the strain, and it is impossible to effect a harmonious combination of the differing cliques. Thus the group falls apart into its various sets and becomes inefficient.

Other men are exactly like that. Now one interest takes the lead in their lives and now another, and there is no way in which the different interests have been built together into a stable system. A period of strain tends to make the divisions between the interests more profound, and once again, though this time for a different reason, the man's character "goes to pieces".

The course of social history has shown perfectly

clearly, however, that if we are to form a genuinely stable social group we must try to keep all the various sources of authority inside the group in close and effective contact one with another. Then, whatever may be the emergency that arises, the one authority most immediately involved can express itself *through* the whole group, and not merely through its own immediate part of the group.

And there are men exactly like this type of group also, with many-sided interests all built together and the connexions between any one and the rest closely and firmly established. To produce that type of character is the aim of all sound education. This man is not one person in sport, another very different person in business; one in command, another, totally different, in subordination; one in peace, another, totally different, in war. Such a man, and only such a man, achieves stability of character and is beyond the reach of mental disease.

If, for the time being, we try to look upon a man as an organisation of different tendencies and interests, just as a group is an organisation of different individuals, we shall very much more easily be able to grasp the principles and causation of mental disease.

Everybody who has written about the psycho-neuroses of warfare has pointed out the extreme difference between the normal, every-day environment of civilised life and that of a fighting force at war. In one sense civilisation may be characterised as an immense conspiracy to make things safe. No doubt when everything possible is done, danger is still common enough. A glance at the accident columns of the daily newspapers is sufficient to prove that this is the case. But danger is not a part of our daily common experience. It lurks unseen, and for the most part unregarded, in many phases of modern life, and one of our great "slogans" in all departments of activity is "Safety First".

Not only is danger hidden, but, for the greater part, so is discomfort. Our ships are "floating palaces"; even the enthusiastic devotee of winter sports must have his magnificent hotel to retire to at night; advertisers tell us, if they want to sell their goods, that their chairs are the easiest chairs, their mattresses the most comfortable mattresses, their cars the last word in luxurious upholstery. When a man adventures abroad, he generally takes the "conducted tour" and has all the worry removed from his own shoulders. We have developed elaborate and concerted ways of guarding against fatigue: limited hours of work, limited speed of work, and methods involving the minimum possible expenditure of effort. In the same way we organise against pain, trying not only to invent special ways of alleviating it when it cannot be avoided, but seeing that as far as possible it shall be avoided. Thus perhaps all that human mechanism by which we meet danger, endure discomfort, bear fatigue, and do not shrink from pain gets but little exercise and grows weak like a flabby muscle. There is, however, not much evidence that this is the case. The fact that the majority of persons prove capable of adapting themselves very rapidly to war conditions, whatever their civilised peaceful life may have been, shows that the ability to meet danger, discomfort, fatigue, and pain still persists and is still remarkably strong. Probably the most fundamental reason why the modern war produces a great crop of mental diseases is not that it is uncivilised, but that it is not uncivilised enough. The trouble is not merely that a man must face danger, but that he must face danger and do nothing; not that he must endure discomfort, but that he must be relatively passive under discomfort; not merely that he must endure fatigue, but that he must get dog-tired in the pursuit of tremendous efforts that never seem to take him, personally, anywhere in particular. He has, in fact, for the most part to sit still and fight, and the two things are somewhat incompatible. Still more difficult is it to be afraid and sit still; and it is these two incompatibilities which are at the bottom of most of the psycho-neuroses of warfare.

I must now try to say precisely what I propose to attempt in the succeeding discussions. It would be out of place for me to endeavour to put forward a detailed description and classification of the mental troubles of warfare. They are exceedingly varied in their expression, and their close study is a matter which none but the specialist either need or can embark upon. What every officer needs to know are some of their most frequent manifestations, their most important predisposing conditions and immediate causes, and a little about the general lines of their treatment before they arrive at really acute phases. To cover them up, to regard them as in any way disgraceful, and either to minimise or to exaggerate their significance represent extremely common and extremely injudicious attitudes. To recognise that they are perfectly normal reactions of certain types of character under the strain of modern warfare, and to be able to treat the sufferers with sympathy and insight during the early stages of their trouble ought to be regarded as a part of the equipment of every officer. This, as I shall show, need not involve any profound knowledge of the technique of modern psychological methods of combating mental disease. It involves only such study of human character and conduct as any man who is to be given command of others ought to be willing and able to undertake.

First, then, I shall indicate briefly the course of a soldier's entirely normal reactions to modern warfare. Secondly I shall discuss the outstanding symptoms of two of the greatest classes of mental troubles to which group-fighting under present-day conditions seems to lead, and shall show, broadly, how these symptoms arise. In the third place I shall explain what can be done by any efficient, but relatively untrained, person to alleviate and perhaps remove the symptoms which, if they are left to run their course unchecked, may work disaster alike to the life of the individual patient and to the *morale* of his group.

Chapter II. THE NORMAL SOLDIER
IN WAR

Tнᴇ initial effect of war upon troops in the field appears to be definitely stimulating. Men who have perhaps been cooped up in towns, cities, or barracks and subjected to an uninteresting daily routine find themselves out-of-doors and under less immediate constraint than usual. Particularly troops coming direct from garrison life are less bothered by trifles of formal discipline, often have a more human relationship with their leaders, in spite of the fact that penalties for disobedience are more severe, and are for the time relatively free from most material anxieties. These things all tend to produce a stimulation of so-called "animal spirits," which rests in part upon excited enthusiasm and in part upon that confidence as to the future which most fighting groups feel at the onset of war. At this stage men may be especially ready to endure difficulties, pain, and fatigue without complaint.

The initial exciting effect passes away very rapidly in many instances; less quickly, but not less inevitably, in others. For the mass of the rank and file of the modern army war is by no means a continuous excitement. There may be comparatively little hard bodily activity, though there is usually abundance of discomfort. External distractions of a conventionally pleasing kind—reading, games, concerts, plays, cinemas and the like—are usually to a large extent cut off, and in their absence men tend to be thrown more and more upon their own inner resources. Modern public education and the conditions of life in large centres of population do little to develop these, and in the result a man finds that he is greatly preoccupied by a very few topics, and very often particularly by thoughts about home, his family, wounds, and death. Preoccupation by few topics, and those for the most part rather dismal ones, tends to produce a kind of intellectual stupidity and stagnation, and there is no doubt that it is perfectly normal, after the initial period of excitement is over, for the better men in a fighting unit to suffer considerable intellectual depression, and for the rest to gravitate towards a condition of lowered activity not far removed from a dull stupidity.

Participation in an active attack may lift a man out of this state, and so, to a lesser degree, may resistance to an attack by the enemy. All observers agree that it is easier and requires less courage to attack than to withstand fire without retaliation,[1] and extreme possession by unpleasant thoughts is apt to be peculiarly intense during much of the disagreeable routine of trench-fighting. It is said that soldiers who have been subjected to this routine for somewhat prolonged periods may acquire an unmis-

---

[1] There are, however, interesting racial differences here. Some races can stand the "passive" type of warfare, but lack the fighting vigour and courage to attack, and especially to use "cold steel."

takeable facial expression of gloom, irony, and disgust, which they do not lose for several days. During bombing attacks very unpleasant physiological disturbances, diarrhoea, nausea, and imaginary unpleasant tastes are common.

Even among soldiers who would be accounted perfectly normal, courage often seems to take two very different forms. One may be called the courage of indifference. It appears to be rendered possible largely by that general diminution of mental activity which I have just mentioned. A man goes into extraordinarily exposed and dangerous places apparently in an indifferent and passive sort of way, as if he fails to realise the danger. This type of courage, common as it is, is not very far from being pathological. The other, an active type, involves the control of normal fear by sentiments and ideals of self-respect, social tradition, and by *morale*. It is characteristic of genuinely normal reactions to warfare that the second type should become more persistent and strong as time goes on. The truly normal or sound soldier also quickly establishes habits of behaviour in dangerous situations, and in these conscious considerations have little or no place.

Normal fear or cowardice is a less easy matter to study. Every ordinary individual experiences anxiety and fear before a battle, or when awaiting a probable attack. The main outward expression of this may be heightened mental and physiological activity, resulting in a temporary restlessness which it is extremely difficult to control. The good soldier gets through this stage fairly rapidly, because he is able to find some positive stimulus leading to definite and controlled behaviour in the very situation which provokes the fear. His anxiety, for example, is transformed as it is built up into an urgent desire to succeed, the latter becoming the leading tendency in the man's life for the time being. The pathological case hangs on to this anxiety and fear longer, so that they come eventually to dominate his entire conduct.

A curious fact belonging to group psychology, motivated undoubtedly by fear, is often observed. Soldiers who behave thoroughly well and gallantly in actual fighting may nevertheless be peculiarly ready to believe and pass on stories of a gruesome and unpleasant nature for which there is very little well-attested evidence. Many of these usually have to do with atrocities committed by the enemy. This is all a part of the heightened suggestibility which is apt to characterise any body of men placed under exciting conditions.

In review of this brief account of normal reactions to modern warfare, it appears that the main points are :

First, a general feeling of exaltation, of increase of freedom, of well-being, based in the main on the fact that a number of customary restraints have been relaxed.

Second, the gradual disappearance of this, mainly by consequence of the removal of the possibility of many common pleasant external distractions.

Third, constant preoccupation by a few rather obtrusive ideas, especially by ideas about home, family, wounds, and death.

Fourth, a life ranging between periods of uninteresting routine and of high and intense activity, the latter periods especially often involving very considerable strain. This strain, if it is prolonged, produces the most dangerous mental state and is characterised by a high degree of emotion.

Normal courage seems to be sometimes the genuine control of fear by ideals and *morale*, and sometimes mere indifference to danger, which is more a matter of intellectual and emotional lethargy than of anything else.

Intense anxiety and fear just before a battle are perfectly normal.

Finally, the whole situation is one in which suggestibility tends to be greatly heightened.

There are undoubtedly important differences in the normal history of the soldier in war according to the particular fighting force to which he belongs. Some of these may perhaps be due ultimately to different national characteristics, and they are worth a greater amount of study than has yet been given to them.

Broadly, the normal man passes through the stages of exhilaration, depression, strain, and finally successfully achieves fairly soon a half ironical, half serious, permanent attitude of "sticking it." In the later stages of a war undoubtedly the exhilaration period tends to become less prominent and may perhaps disappear altogether. The really dangerous phase, from the point of view of nervous and mental breakdown, is the period of depression and strain, and it is to a study of this and of its possible results that we must now turn.

Chapter III. CONVERSION HYSTERIA

THERE is as yet no general agreement with regard to the most satisfactory method of classifying the mental troubles of warfare.[1] In their actual symptoms such troubles, whether in war or civil life, are apt to appear extraordinarily diverse, and in consequence numerous classifications have been proposed, in all of which a very considerable amount of overlapping of different alleged mental abnormalities occurs. Since in the present book I cannot pretend to attempt anything approaching a detailed study of this complicated topic, I shall merely indicate the main character and causation of two of the great groups of mental troubles of war: conversion hysteria and anxiety neurosis, as they are commonly called.

Broadly speaking, hysteria is a name given to a form of mental disease in which a person thinks, acts, and feels as if only one, or only a few, of the many tendencies which make up his normal personality were actually in operation. Conversion

[1] In this and the following chapters on mental disabilities I shall deal with principles rather than with details. The best short study of the mental disorders of warfare available and more or less suitable to the general reader is *War Neuroses*, by J. T. MacCurdy, Cambridge, 1918. Rather more popular is *Shell Shock*, by Prof. G. Elliot Smith and Prof. T. H. Pear, Manchester, 1919. An interesting account of the after-history of a good number of neurotic cases is to be found in *Shell Shock and its Aftermath*, by Norman Fenton, London, 1926.

hysteria is the name given to a particular form of this disease in which the patient appears to have some definite bodily injury or disability, although as a matter of fact the root of the trouble is that certain of his mental tendencies have escaped from control and are playing an altogether predominant part in the determination of his conduct. In conversion hysteria, that is, a mental abnormality is converted into, or at least is finding expression in, a bodily symptom.

As we have seen, the initial effect of war is normally exhilarating; but this effect is temporary and soon gives place to depression and strain, as a result of which the soldier tends to be especially preoccupied with a few thoughts and particularly with topics concerning his home and family and the risks of fighting. Now we might say that from thinking about being wounded a man goes on to act as if he were wounded, though as a matter of fact he is not, and that whenever this occurs we have a case of conversion hysteria. Then we could say that the whole of conversion hysteria is simply an illustration of the natural issue of ideas in some form of bodily activity. But this would be seriously wrong. First, there is no real reason to believe that ideas ever *do* naturally issue in action; second, there is the fact that many men think often and intensely about wounds who do not act as if they are wounded; and third, there is the fact, which must be explained, of the tremendous variety of symptoms which conversion hysteria may show.

I shall therefore take a few hypothetical, but essentially realistic, illustrations in order to demonstrate the sort of process which does actually happen.

Here is a man who is extremely good at all kinds of vigorous games. He decides upon a career success in which demands unimpaired bodily activity. All goes well until one day his leg is badly injured in an accident. For a time it looks as if his career will be completely ruined. Now we may assume that the whole of his life tends to centre on success in this one chosen sphere of activity. All his interests are bound up in that, and if that fails he has little or nothing in reserve. It is a not uncommon case. The accident is naturally a great blow to the man. He resents it. He cannot build it in with his scheme of things. For the time being he tends to look upon life as essentially unjust and unfair. The accident and its consequences cannot be fitted into the plan of life which he has elaborately constructed, and they remain outside the main stream of his interests. However, he makes an unexpectedly complete recovery. He resumes his old career, and the accident now remains a mere incident, still outside the things that go to make up the stream of his regular waking life. He rarely or never thinks of it.

War breaks out. In one important respect it is like the old accident over again. It, also, threatens to ruin his career. He cannot fit it in with the general trend of his success. Nevertheless he desires to play his part, and goes to the fight. The initial excitement over, he, as usual, becomes depressed. The depression may be unusually deep. It is like the depression which followed the accident. He can escape from it only in the old way : by resuming his career. If he could get a disabling wound that would take him out of the war but would, like the old leg trouble, not finally interrupt his life-work, all would yet be well. But he tries to prevent himself from thinking about that, because even to think of it is a kind of cowardice or disloyalty. Nevertheless the idea is there, hardly formed, never clearly expressed, but backed up by an intense interest in a special career into which the war and all that belongs to it cannot readily be fitted. One day a shell bursts near him and a bit of earth strikes his leg. He is not badly hurt. He walks back to his post, but when he wakes the next morning he finds that he is lame. His leg is as if it were paralysed. He has become a conversion hysteric.

This is an exact history of many such cases. It was not merely contemplating the idea of the wound that upset the man. Very intimately connected with the idea were all the strong interests bearing upon his career. He became hysterical, not because he got a certain idea, but because in that organisation of interests which constituted his normal personality there was no room for the war, or for anything else that would threaten to ruin his cherished ambitions. At the same time it must be remembered that it was his leg which appeared to be paralysed. If in the original accident his arm had been hurt, it might have been the arm now; if his eyes, he might have gone functionally blind; if his hearing, he might have seemed to be deaf, and so on. There is practically always, or it may be always, some fact of past history which explains the direction taken by the symptom, although the emergence of the symptom is due directly to a present mental conflict.

Such an account seems fairly clear for the case of the man whose whole life revolves around one outstanding interest. But what about the far more common case of the person who has no one outstanding interest or group of interests dominating his daily conduct? He acts according to the dictates of the moment. Most people live a fairly routine life, in which one interest follows another according to a regularly arranged and regularly varying environment, and the various interests involved neither conflict violently with one another nor are organised together to any extent. Such a man is like a very loosely organised group in which the various cliques or sets play their parts without much relation to the rest, and do not come much into touch one with another.

Suppose this type of man goes into the fighting-line. He shares the initial exaltation and the following depression. As always, he tends to be pursued by ideas of home and wounds. It is not the fact that these ideas, merely as ideas, come to him that is important. If that were all, he might just as well be pursued by ideas of a good meal, or of a football match, for they are very likely to represent equally prominent features of his daily life. Thoughts of home and of wounds are obsessive because they present to him ways of escape from danger. It is his lifelong habit to react to the immediately presented situation in terms of the simple impulse most immediately awakened. But he is not allowed to do this now. Discipline prevents him. If he did so react, he would desert, and that means almost certain drastic punishment, whereas the chances of war are at least a little uncertain. There is, however, for such a man no way by which the fear of the danger of fighting can be taken up into some mental tendency larger and more powerful than itself. His ambition cannot deal with it, for he has none or very little. His self-respect is not strong enough to cope with it, for all his life he has followed a policy of drift. He has no ideal strong and stable enough to control these immediate tendencies towards an easy method of escape. He must therefore continually live in a situation which produces tremendously strong impulses to get out of it, but which at the same time provides no simple mechanism by which escape may be compassed. It is this relatively uncontrolled impulse to escape which is at the back of the ideas of wounds and home. Some day, it may be suddenly, by the bursting of a shell, by the violent death of a friend, or perhaps with no such obvious immediate cause, the wound which solves his conflict appears. It is not really a bodily wound. It takes a bodily form, but his body is sound enough. He has become hysterical. We call him a conversion hysteric because an impulse to escape, which is mental, has found expression, or become converted into, a bodily symptom. The symptom usually follows the line of some old-standing weakness, or it may be directly connected with his present work, as when a sniper goes blind or suffers a one-sided paralysis, or a look-out man gets a twisted neck, or an interpreter goes dumb, or a hydrophone-listener becomes deaf. In other cases, again, the particular symptom may be due to some actual physical shock, as when loss of voice follows gassing; or to the fact that the patient once knew somebody who displayed some peculiar symptom and who is more or less closely connected with his present situation. A special case of the last type is where the patient actually acts as if he were somebody else whom, at some time in his past life, he has ardently wished to be like. But this last case is perhaps somewhat less common in war than in civil life.

It is now possible to formulate a general explanation of all these abnormalities. Whenever we have to meet a new situation in life, we must try to link the impulses, feelings, and ideas especially connected with this situation on to others belonging to the past, and somehow to build them together so that they all achieve adequate and harmonious expression. This is sometimes a task too difficult, as when a sudden, overwhelming grief is thrown into a hitherto happy existence, or when a deadly and persistent fear comes into a life in which fear has played only a very little and incidental part. If the person is naturally tender-hearted or timid, the difficulty is all the greater. Then adaptation to the situation is incomplete. A person outwardly may act as if nothing important has happened, but all the time incompatible tendencies, with their connected ideas and feelings, are at work within him, and they may, in the end, break through to open expression. If they do, the result is hysteria.

It is an essential fact about the patient suffering from conversion hysteria that he does not very vigorously fight against his fears. He is, on the whole, the type of man whose instincts have to fight out a difficulty amongst themselves and are not under the control of some stable sentiment or ideal which is within the man, and not outside him. We have already seen that it ought to be the object of some part of army training to develop such inner control, and in so far as this attempt is genuinely successful, conversion hysteria is guarded against. So long, however, as the fear of danger can be controlled only by fear of a greater danger, which is just so long as discipline, in the strict sense of the word, and not *morale*, is the ground of a man's conduct, the attempt to establish ideals of loyalty and the like has failed, and there is fruitful material for the production of conversion hysteria. To this is due, in great measure, the fact, first, I believe, emphasised by Dr J. T. MacCurdy, but fairly generally admitted now, that in the late war, so far

as the British forces were concerned, the incidence
of conversion hysteria was relatively greatest among
the rank and file, while so-called "anxiety neuroses"
were relatively more frequent among officers, and
among the better class of officers too. In fact a conversion case may not even realise that any conflict
preceded his trouble at all[1]. He has had his thoughts
of home and of wounds and his longings for both.
But why should he not have? These represent the
obvious and respectable ways out of danger.

[1] Cf. *Functional Nerve Diseases,* ed. Crichton Miller, Oxford,
1920, 57.

Chapter IV. ANXIETY NEUROSIS

ANXIETY neurosis is not something totally different from conversion hysteria. It results from very much the same external conditions, but in its final form it is a graver, more obstinate, more deeply rooted disorder.

One way of making a distinction, though not, probably, a very good one, is to say that conversion hysteria is a veiled attempt to escape from an intolerable present danger, whereas anxiety neurosis results from a dread of some intolerable danger that is as yet not fully realised and that belongs to a probable future. Thus in the last war a considerable number of men who were perfectly happy in training-camps far from the seat of fighting collapsed when once they got on board a troop-ship and set out oversea. For then, though no enemy had as yet been sighted, they imagined themselves open to submarine attacks. It was the anxiety consequent upon an anticipatory fear that stimulated the collapse, and the breakdown itself was apt to be general rather than expressed in some relatively isolated and localised bodily disability. However, this kind of anxiety state, though it may temporarily render a man totally useless for fighting, has to be distinguished from the true anxiety neurosis, where the collapse is profound and deep-seated, and is apt to be of very long duration and difficult to remove.

It is in view of this that a differentiation between conversion hysteria and anxiety neurosis resting upon the degree to which a threatened patient fights against the oncoming breakdown is often proposed. The conversion hysteric is the man who submits easily and is willing to accept the relatively easy way out—a slight bodily disablement. To some men who are threatened by mental disaster a far more serious problem is set. They have strong ideals of duty, of service to their country, of personal or collective honour, and of responsibility, in many cases, to the men whom they have to lead. They therefore wage a great struggle against what they regard as the dishonourable thoughts of an easy way to safety. If they find, as most men do, that when once the initial excitement of war is over they begin to be obsessed by thoughts of home, of friends, and eventually of wounds, they forcibly drive such thoughts from their minds. In this way they may succeed in passing through the critical period of depression, and in adapting themselves to the dangerous and disagreeable conditions of warfare.

Most men, in fact, do achieve such adaptation. For one thing, the human organism is extraordinarily capable of setting up new habits, and if a habit can be established, although the circumstances which led up to it may have been disagreeable in the extreme, those circumstances become less and less noticeable as the habit becomes more and more firmly established. If the modern war of position imposes in many ways a more intolerable strain than the old war of movement, it is, on the other hand, much more easily dealt with by the establishment of a routine way of life, and this again in most cases tends to dull the soldier's conscious appreciation of discomfort and strain. Not only the establishment of habit, but in many instances the influence of ambition and of a capacity to command lessen the dangerous effects of preoccupation with dismal forebodings and take control of the fear of danger and the shrinking from discomfort, and so assist a man through the most difficult periods of his war career.

In some instances, however, a man's conscientiousness forbids him even to think about wounds as a way of escape from danger, and responsibility only heightens his fear of ultimate collapse. Everybody is familiar with the same kind of thing so far as certain bodily injuries are concerned. Different people are very differently sensitive to pain. One man with a slightly strained or torn muscle will give up at once, rest, and recover quickly. Another man with the same degree of injury will simply set his teeth and continue as usual. When this man finally does break down, he suffers badly, and it may take him a long time to recover. In the same way the man who fights strenuously against an advancing mental breakdown in general suffers all the more severely if eventually he is subdued.

We have seen how everybody who has been used to a normal, modern, civilised environment will naturally wish to get away from discomfort and danger. But to a highly conscientious person there is only one way out which is consistent with honour. Here I shall follow MacCurdy closely in support of a view for which he himself is mainly responsible. In some cases the mental make-up of a soldier tends to make the early fears of warfare, which are perfectly normal, unduly intense and unduly prolonged. There sets in a persistent and inescapable fatigue, which is partly physiological as the result of long hours of duty, arduous toil, and irregular meals, and partly psychological as a result of the necessity for constant alertness under difficulty. The soldier now begins to lose some of those capacities which in ordinary life we all show without ever thinking about them: his sense of direction, his power to control bodily movements accurately. He may have momentary, swiftly passing attacks of giddiness. He does not know which way a shell which he can hear is coming. Every shell he hears seems as if it may have been aimed at him personally, and the strain of a heavy bombardment is terrific. At this stage ideas of escape become pressing.

There are [says MacCurdy] three practicable avenues of escape; the man may receive an incapacitating wound, he may be taken prisoner, or he may be killed. One who manifests an anxiety state is always one with high ideals of his duty. We find therefore that none of them entertain the hope of disabling wounds. Nor do they consciously seek surrender, but it is interesting that they not infrequently dream of it at this stage. The third possibility is the most alluring, as it offers complete release and is quite compatible with all standards of duty.[1]

Thus, gradually but irresistibly, the desire for death is built up. The man may then actually plan to be killed, but always so that it will appear that he could not have avoided his death. Or he may on the spur of the moment appear recklessly brave. "Once the desire for death has become fixed, the breakdown is imminent."

Even now there generally has to be some final accident to bring about the collapse. This may be a sudden near-by explosion, the sight of the death of a friend, burial by earth thrown up by an exploding shell, or, it may be, merely the withdrawal unexpectedly of a promised leave or the sudden curtailment of a leave. The things that may appear finally to lead to the breakdown are many and very varied, but they are only the final events of a long history. Hardly ever does a real wound lead to a neurosis, for the real wound solves the conflict upon which the mental trouble is based, so that there is no longer any immediate reason for psychological disturbance.

The actual acute symptoms of the anxiety state as it occurs in warfare need not concern us very much, and I shall therefore describe them only very briefly. At first, commonly, there is a state of stupor, which may involve genuine loss of con-

[1] *Op. cit.* 23.

sciousness. For the time being the patient is almost as if he were really dead. When this passes away, usually the patient is excited, confused, does not know where he is, often cannot find his way from place to place, may complain of violent headaches and may be delirious, usually raving about enemy attacks. In other cases there may be no loss of consciousness, but the patient may be unable to produce voluntary movement and may be confused, unusually forgetful, and apparently unable to talk. Very often indeed hallucinations occur at this stage, that is to say vivid imaginings which are confused with reality. These generally have to do with enemy aggression. Now also is the stage of extraordinarily vivid nightmare, accompanied by fear of a peculiarly intense type. These dreams, by inducing fear of sleep, increase fatigue. Tremors, uncontrollable quivering of a limb or of the limbs, are often present, and any degree of bright light is apt to be exceedingly distressing. Patients suffering from anxiety neurosis are frequently more than normally unsociable. During the earlier phases they have been much wrapped up in themselves, and to that degree cut off from their fellows; in the more acute stages this is more than usually intensified.

The acute stages of anxiety generally last for two or three weeks, but, particularly where proper treatment is not available, they may continue for months. Gradually the symptoms abate and become less violent, or more intermittent. The nightmares cease to be wholly occupied with themes of warfare. The man who has so far dreamed about being blown up by a shell may now dream of being run over by a train or by a motor-car. Bit by bit the dreams themselves come to have a less terrible ending. For a long time the patient is unusually easily fatigued and remains "jumpy." Any sudden unexpected sound or any sight that may remind him of the war provokes a temporary relapse. In the end there may be the bodily reaction without the accompanying actual experience of fear. "I was talking to a patient," says MacCurdy, "when he moved to knock some ashes from a cigarette into a small bowl. While his hand was approaching the bowl a door slammed. The patient proceeded to execute his movement quite carefully and then to jump violently, although more than a second had elapsed between the sound and the jump." It does not by any means follow that a patient who appears normal can be said to be fit for trench-warfare again. Usually he is not, and if he were sent back, there would soon be a recurrence of all the old symptoms. Almost invariably the period of recovery is accompanied by deep and persistent dejection.

So much, in brief, for the general character and symptoms of anxiety neurosis. It is more important for us to study the predisposing causes and the kind of mental characteristics which are likely to lead to nervous disease under modern war conditions. To this study I shall turn in the next chapter.

Chapter V. PREDISPOSING CONDITIONS

It is a matter of the greatest interest and importance to study the general conditions which predispose a man towards mental breakdown under the conditions of modern warfare, so far as these can be stated in terms of his own personality. These conditions are, in fact, important not only in relation to war. There is no disease of a mental order peculiar to warfare and not found at all in civilian life. But the strain and the mental conflict which produce the mental disorders of civil life are naturally due to different external circumstances. In both cases the root cause is to be found in lack of adaptation between a man's character and the conditions under which he is forced to live. In civil life the difficulty usually arises from the fact that certain social conventions, or certain necessary conduct forced upon him by some thoroughly distasteful job which, nevertheless, he cannot escape from by any recognised means, set up an intolerable mental strain. In war the ultimate reason is that conditions which are, in fact, abnormal put an abnormal strain upon little exercised activities. Thus perhaps it is true to say that the war cases follow, as a rule, a more uniform course. In war, as in peace, however, the trouble arises from a profound incompatibility between circumstances and character. There is a type of personality which can triumphantly survive such incompatibility, and there is another type which cannot do this. We have now to try to understand what makes a man unable to withstand that kind of incompatibility which war almost invariably produces.

Cases of mental breakdown nearly always have a long history, and the more stubborn and profound they are, the more is this certain to be true. There is no such thing as a sudden collapse into an anxiety neurosis. Take the case of a young officer with whom I had a good deal to do during the late years of the last war. He was a very bad case of anxiety neurosis. A great amount, though of course not the whole, of his difficulty began when, as a small, clever, but nervous boy at a preparatory school he was often dragged out in front of his class by a stupid teacher as a "star" performer. He was then told that if he made mistakes, or broke down, in what he was required to do, everybody would laugh at him. Gradually there had grown up in him an attitude towards life in virtue of which every difficulty was for him the sort of problem in which he would probably break down and become a laughing-stock. It was no wonder that the increasing responsibilities of his somewhat brilliant war career produced eventually a state of hopeless collapse. His difficulties were not, however, essentially war difficulties. They started long before the war and could have been avoided by judicious pre-war training. And his was not an isolated case.

Thus it is of extraordinary importance that a

man's predispositions in this direction should be considered carefully when he "joins up," or decides upon a career in the army. Nobody can predict, except in certain relatively outstanding cases, that a man assuredly will have a breakdown if he goes into war, but precautions can, and should, be taken to avoid the chance of one, either by keeping a man out of certain careers or by directing his choice of the kind of work that is to be done within a given career.

Obviously any man who has already suffered a nervous breakdown should avoid any career which will put him into conditions of life at all similar to those which produced the trouble. He may have made what looks like a perfect recovery, but he is likely to be more or less permanently unstable in certain directions. Very often no enquiries are made about this matter, and thereby a serious injustice may be done to the individual and a serious source of danger introduced into his group.

A man who, as a child, was very subject to night terrors and fear of the dark is, in general, liable to panic of a greater than normal intensity, and rarely makes a good soldier on active service. In particular, a childish fear of thunderstorms, of an intense kind, is apt to develop into definite mental collapse in the adult under conditions of intense bombardment.

Many men suffer a small degree of discomfort whenever they are placed in confined spaces. In going down a subway they experience a slight shrinking. They would rather climb laboriously up hundreds of steps than enter a lift. Even during the climb they are unhappy if the staircase is narrow and enclosed, and they hurry to get out of it, escaping with what to other people seems an exaggerated relief. They may have been troubled by nightmares of premature burial, or of being uncomfortably confined in a narrow space. All these are symptoms of what is technically known as "claustrophobia," or fear of confined areas, and they are apt to break out very violently in trench warfare, for trenches and dug-outs are generally narrow and enclosed. The alternative to a dug-out is often an exposed area where the chance of violent death is considerable. Yet a good many men during the late war preferred the reasonable fear of death in the open to the apparently unreasonable fear of burial in the enclosed dug-out.

A very important predisposing condition is an unusual degree of shyness, or lack of sociability, or secretiveness. This may arise from all kinds of different causes which are too numerous and too varied for me to discuss here. It greatly unfits a man to deal satisfactorily with the ordinary situations of daily life, since most of these demand a fairly high degree of social adaptiveness. In warfare a man who shuts himself up within himself is thereby greatly increasing his liability to mental disturbance. He has, as MacCurdy says, "less of an outlet for his feelings in the trenches, and is less distracted from the thoughts of the painfulness of his situation than is his normal companion. As a result he becomes more quickly a prey to all the influences that generate fatigue and dissatisfaction."[1]

Even if these predisposing conditions have been present in a man's past life, it is not certain that he will break down in war. He may have attained a stability of character sufficient to surmount without disaster all but the most severe shocks. Again, there may be no available evidence of these predisposing conditions, and yet a man may break down readily. Everything depends ultimately upon whether there are important and strong tendencies in his character which are relatively dissevered from the rest. If there are, and the environment puts a strain upon these, they will fail him. The kind of reactions the weakness or isolation of which are most of all likely to be found out by a war environment are those which I have just mentioned : fears of dark, of thunderstorms, of enclosed spaces, of solitude and the like. A little judicious questioning and examination by a man whose business it is to understand mental reactions would usually bring out any marked bias in any of these directions which a candidate for army service might possess.

To know predisposing conditions and to know what to do as a result of them are two very different things. Secretiveness and lack of sociability apart, they are all likely seriously to hinder a man only after war has broken out, and even then only under certain conditions of acute strain. Thus it is

[1] *Op. cit.* 34.

less important to be able to detect them when it is a question of building up a peace-time establishment, or of fighting of the rather open and active character.

Moreover some of these predisposing conditions are much more common than we usually realise. Night terrors in childhood, for instance, fear of heavy sounds, or of great heights, and a shrinking from narrowly confined spaces are all found very frequently indeed. They could hardly be made a ground for refusing a man admittance to the Army. Further, once a war has begun and the demand for men is insistent, to excuse men with this kind of mental "kink" and fear would obviously be dangerous, since the evidence for them at admission, except in the most unmistakeable cases, is bound to rest mainly on the word of the man himself. It is certain that more careful enquiries concerning mental characteristics and disabilities ought to be made when a man joins the army. It is certain also that these ought to be made by persons possessing psychological knowledge and skill. But it is only in the extreme cases, I think, that the occurrence of such disabilities should be made a definite bar to entrance. They should as far as possible always be known, and they should be given consideration when the branch of service suitable to a given candidate is being determined.

Now this means that the duty of dealing with predisposing conditions of mental breakdown, so as, if possible, to prevent them from developing further, must belong to the ordinary army officer, and particularly to the grade of officer who is most immediately in touch with the individual men. It is in many ways easier to deal with a potential mental invalid than with a man who has already badly broken down. In many such cases it is not necessary, in order to treat them successfully, to have a very profound knowledge of psychology. We must take some trouble to understand how emotional expression and various forms of almost compulsive behaviour can be set up. The very process of understanding how they are established often indicates how they can be treated, if, in individual cases, they should take forms and directions that run against the general interest. To a study of methods of alleviation of these mental troubles therefore, in so far as such methods may be practised safely by a person who is in no sense a special mental physician, we must now turn our attention.

Chapter VI. METHODS OF TREATMENT

THIS is not the place to attempt any detailed exposition of the various technical methods which are used in the treatment of nervous and mental breakdown. They are essentially the concern of the man who, with an adequate general medical training, has specialised on the mental side of disease. Our concern is rather how a person who is known to have some predisposition towards mental trouble can be treated so as to render such trouble less likely or perhaps impossible. Such treatment is merely a matter of common sense directed by a certain amount of psychological insight and is within the powers of most people to apply at least to some extent. I shall keep in mind throughout not so much the patient who has broken down as the person who, unless he is intelligently guided in the control of his erring and relatively isolated tendencies, may, and in all probability will, break down.

There is one striking characteristic about all the predisposing conditions of which I have spoken: they are all *fears* of one kind or another—fear of excessive and sudden noise, fear of confined spaces, fear of society, or fears which are perhaps all the more intense because their object cannot be very definitely named. Now the great majority of these fears have been produced by some special features of experience, by misdirected education, or by the persistent effect of social tradition. The very young

child seems to display the characteristic fear-behaviour under two sets of conditions only: when a
sudden loud sound is made to break in upon him while
he is resting quietly or is interested in something
else; and when bodily support is suddenly removed.
It is sometimes urged, on the basis of this observation, that these two fears alone are "natural" or
instinctive to human-kind.[1] This does not follow in
the least. It seems certain that in the human animal
there is a normal order of development, in the course
of which many situations, originally indifferent or un-
appreciated, provoke fear-reactions just as naturally
and inevitably as the original sudden noise and removal of support.

Two things, however, are important. The first is
that special fears, narrowly tied up with particular
circumstances, and also abnormally intense fears
almost invariably have their origin in some particular, though often many times repeated, fact of
experience. The second is that the original, natural,
or instinctive fears themselves can be controlled
and prevented from having evil mental effects, even
though they should occur in people who have a
naturally timid kind of temperament.

It is worth while taking an illustration or two to
show how special fears may grow up, both as a result of experimental conditions and in the course
of every-day life.

If a human infant, a few months old, who has so
far been kept away from all furry animals is suddenly
confronted by a rat, or a guinea-pig, or a small dog,

[1] J. B. Watson, *Behaviorism*, London, 1925, 121–2.

or a cat, he is usually very readily attracted by the animal's movements, looks at it, shows, normally, no signs of shrinking, and often actually stretches out towards the animal to play with it. It can be arranged that on several successive occasions, every time the animal is presented, a sudden loud unfamiliar noise is simultaneously produced. The noise naturally gives rise to shrinking and perhaps crying. After a while, when the animal alone is put before the infant, he reacts to it, in many cases, just as if the sound were there, that is to say, he shows all the characteristic signs of fright. He no longer stretches out his hand towards the animal, but draws away, if he is old enough crawls away, and often cries loudly. The fear, originally specific to the noise, has become attached to the animal, and may, particularly if it is not counteracted by older people, remain attached to the animal for long periods. It should not be assumed that this apparent transfer of fear occurs merely because the sight of the animal accompanied the sound of the sudden noise. There are, no doubt, other conditions as well, as for instance that the baby must be specially interested in the animal while the sound is actually being produced. Leaving this out of consideration for the moment, the fact remains that a special fear has been experimentally produced, where originally no fear whatsoever was manifested. This experiment has several times been performed with success.[1]

Next we may return to the case which I have

[1] For a full account see Watson, *op. cit.* Lecture VIII.

already mentioned, of the man who, from being abnormally anti-social and suspicious of other people, developed a bad attack of anxiety during the late war. As a small, rather undersized, but very intelligent boy at school he was often brought out in front of his class to demonstrate to visitors how well the pupils were taught. "If you make mistakes," said his teacher, "they will all laugh at you." Like everybody else, he did make mistakes sometimes and suffered the promised penalty. His case was no doubt a very complex one, but in a large measure, out of these early experiences developed a persistent notion that society is an organisation "to let a man down," to make capital out of a man's mistakes. "Everybody must stand by himself" was his attitude to life. Thus there grew up a pronounced anti-social tendency and a fear of other people.

In the same way abnormally intense fears almost invariably have a special history. It is a common experience to meet with people who are uneasy or even definitely frightened during thunderstorms. I knew a case in which, during childhood, a boy suffered very abnormal and intense fear in a thunder-storm. To some extent this may be regarded as in no way unusual, since sudden, unfamiliar, and unprepared-for noises generally produce fear-behaviour. But it is uncommon for fear of thunder to persist and remain extremely intense for long. The noise, like other noises, soon becomes fairly familiar and then ceases to produce any very marked effect.

This boy, however, had a grandmother who lived near to his own home, and who suffered from an excessive terror of thunder. As soon as a storm promised or came, she would rush to the boy's home and display the most lively fear. Long before he can talk, or even understand language, a child is very responsive to any exhibition of apprehensiveness in his elders. When that boy learned to understand words, he heard his grandmother talk of sudden death, of wickedness, and of the Day of Judgment whenever a thunder-storm happened to occur. These were all things which in his home, and in the books that were given to him, he was taught to dread, and these were the things that kept alive and intensified his normal fear, rendering it abnormal. That is the exact history of a great many of these special fears. We take them over from a social environment which is crowded with them. It does not matter how they grew up in the first place. They are now ready-made, to be assimilated by the impressionable child.

One of the first and most important of the tasks to be attempted by anyone who desires to correct these special fears is to discover something about their history in the individual who suffers from them. If the way in which they originated can be made clear, much can be learned as to how they can be successfully counteracted. There are some people, indeed, who go so far as to say that if we can explain their individual origin, that is to say if we can convince the patient that there is a reasonable explanation of his fears the difficulty will clear up of itself. This is probably never literally true, and it certainly is not true of fears of long standing. However, to find out how they grew up in the individual is to get at least half the clue as to how they may be removed, should removal be possible.

It is of little use to lay down any hard and fast rules about how to lay bare this past history. The methods must vary from individual to individual, and with the character of the person who is conducting the enquiry. Clues may often be discovered from dreams, for, as everybody knows, in the dream incidents that have been completely overlaid and forgotten in ordinary waking life may find direct or symbolic representation. Once the trail has been started, a great amount of further information may be obtained by the method which is now widely known as "free association." Lists of words are prepared, some of which are relatively indifferent to the particular patient concerned, and some of which are obviously related to the incidents or class of incidents which are suspected to be involved in the development of the abnormal fears. The patient is placed as much at his ease as possible and is instructed that when he hears any given word read to him he is to respond with the first word that comes into his mind, without any critical consideration of what he is doing. The times taken by the patient to respond and the nature of the associated words which he gives are then carefully studied, and from these further clues are almost invariably forthcoming.

In some cases personal antipathy, which is extremely common in patients suffering from nervous and mental trouble, will develop, and prevent a particular investigator from ever scoring any real success. He must then at once recognise his incapacity and, if possible, turn over the enquiry to somebody else. In general what are required are sympathy, great patience, imagination, and a genuine interest in human life and conduct. What I have called the "institutional" type of officer will never be any good at this kind of job, and he had better admit that fact from the beginning.

The important question is how to remove the danger from these fears, whether or not their individual history is discovered.

The commonest and certainly the worst method is the "sink or swim" method of the martinet. I knew a man who, being very fearful of high places, forced himself every day to climb up the perpendicular face of a large building by hanging on to small projecting pieces of masonry. He became much worse. Most people would do so. There is extraordinarily little evidence for the view that any strong tendency whatever can be reduced to insignificance *merely* by habituation. If the tendency is of moderate strength only, the matter is different. The fear, for example, in such a case is already to some extent controlled; there are, that is, other important elements in the mental attitude to the dangerous situation of the person concerned, and by repetition these other elements may come to take the lead. The fear is then, not indeed removed, but kept under, so that it definitely helps to render the situation one which is dealt with in a duly cautious manner. Thus the reckless man is either the person who is so terrifically afraid that he will do anything to escape from his fear, or else the person who does not notice that there is any danger in the situation whatsoever. The plan of forcing a man to face extreme degrees of the very thing he most fears is generally silly and wholly unpsychological.

Let us return to the case of the experimentally produced fear of animals. It is claimed that such experimentally produced fear can be perfectly well experimentally removed. The conditions required are that when the animal is presented, simultaneously some new interest should be aroused in such a way that this new interest is tied up with the old fear. Young children commonly display a great amount of mutual emulation. "What he can do, I can do" is a common attitude. Accordingly an animal is produced and the usual acquired shrinking and apparent fear follow. But another child is brought in who has not learned this fear. He takes up the animal and fondles it. No obvious bad effects follow. When this has happened a few times, the frightened child again seems to become interested in the animal, may stretch out towards it, take it up and handle it, and so may apparently recover from his fear. The observations that have actually been made are not sufficiently detailed and careful at this point. I should expect that the child still remains more or less on guard, more wary than he was at first. The fear has now lost its compulsive character, however, for it has been combined with a different interest, and as a result has become transformed.

No doubt the long-standing fears which may issue in an anxiety state are nothing like so easily dealt with, but the general condition for their successful treatment is precisely the same. They have somehow to be built together with some positive interest, which then does not merely control them but actually changes their character.

I will take two very common cases and try to show some of the ways in which this transformation may be effected.

Here is a man with a long-standing intense fear of thunder-storms. He enters the army, proceeds on active service, and may have to stand the strain of a heavy bombardment, a strain which for him may be a thousand times more difficult to endure than for his more normal companions. In practically all such cases, however, the fear of thunder is not equally present under all circumstances. It is greater at night than in the day-time, in solitude than in company, in idleness than in work. It is perhaps least of all when the man is with somebody whom he regards as more fragile, weaker, more generally timid than himself. The patient will say truly that under these circumstances it is not that the fear is, by a tremendous effort on his part, prevented from finding expression. His whole attitude towards the storm is different from what it was, and very often there is no fear at all. If only this attitude can be made permanent, the fear is conquered, in the sense that it now has no chance of breaking through and producing dangerous states of mind or of body. It is not, of course, altogether easy to cope with the case of the thunder-storm, for storms often come when they are not expected and are not arranged by the devices of man. But the bombardment situation may be in some respects a little easier. So far as possible it ought to be arranged that a man of the type likely to suffer dangerous mental strain should get his early experiences of heavy shelling under conditions in which his fear of similar sounds is least of all noticeable.

Early impressions are profoundly important in almost all forms of human conduct, for once an attitude is adopted, it is apt to be remarkably persistent and to change much less than the circumstances of the situation in which it is evoked. The most important thing of all, however, is that the attitude finally set up should not depend to any high degree upon mere attendant circumstances, but upon facts belonging to the character of the man himself. For example, a man who has developed a profound interest in beauty in nature may actually find his attitude to a storm changed entirely by this, and his fear of it lost in admiration of its beauty.

Somehow or other, whenever there is any special fear, it has to be linked with the strongest positive interest of a healthy character in the man's life, and in this way it will be transformed. What particular interest can be thus utilised varies from man to man, and so it is not possible to lay down any general laws of procedure which apply in all cases. There must in any instance be a sympathetic insight into the character of the man concerned. A man may have no such commanding and suitable interest. Then one must be built up. He may have the kind of temperament in which such an interest cannot be built up. The sooner such a man gets removed from an army, or put into some branch of a service which will not stir up his special fears, the better.

Take another case, the case of the abnormally secretive, anti-social person. As before, a beginning must be made by the attempt to find out the particular circumstances which gave rise to his lack of sociability. These are extraordinarily varied, but they tend to centre upon some incident or period in the course of which the patient was " let down " by somebody for whom he had a great respect or a great love, or by some class of people towards whom his attitude was somewhat submissive. The next step is to discover what are that man's actual positive interests. It is a fortunate fact that there are remarkably few interests that cannot in some way or other be better satisfied by social co-operation than in solitude. Our man will have concentrated upon these few. His work may force him

into contact with others whom he regards as irksome
and intolerable. As soon as he is free of it, he goes
off fishing, or shuts himself up in a study, or plays
a solitary game of golf. Even in golf, however, he
cannot escape bogey, and books are a kind of
friends, and the fisherman, after his solitary performance, often likes to tell tales. Something can
almost always be found, within any type of interest,
that a man can satisfy best when he is with other
people. The plan of campaign is to work upon that.
It is a difficult business, for both sides have to be
delicately humoured, the solitary man rarely being
regarded as a desirable companion. But gradually,
by the choice of the right people and the stimulation of the right interests, it is possible to merge
the fear in something else, and so to produce a new
attitude and to guard against impending disaster.

By whatever detailed treatment the change is
effected, the principle is always the same, and it is
this: whenever in human life two or more interests
are built together, so that they no longer operate
in isolation, a new mental attitude is produced.
Only actual study of specific cases will lay bare the
laws of this process of mental construction and so
tell us beforehand what sort of effect is likely to
be produced when any two or more given interests
are synthesised.

Thus this study of the general method by which
the predisposing conditions of mental breakdown
should be combated leads us back to the position
which I have already several times stated. Stable

mental health depends directly upon the degree to which all the prominent interests in a man's life are built together. If an interest of any kind breaks away from, or is never assimilated to, the main mass of the man's interests and begins to operate by itself, there is danger.

When any soldier goes into action, he is apt to get into a state of general commotion. Instincts, and interests break partially out of control and threaten to run riot. After a while these erring tendencies appear to be reorganised. The centre of the man's mental life has shifted somewhat. Instead of making everything subordinate to getting a rise of wages next year, say, he subordinates everything to getting a rise of rank. He is then, in current psychological terminology, said to have " sublimated " his dangerous tendencies. But this is merely an imposing way of saying that a difficult mental period has, permanently or for the time being, been satisfactorily passed. Whether in the normal case or in the abnormal case, the passing in this manner of such a dangerous period brings into play the same sort of mechanism. Tendencies which were threatening or had achieved independent action, have been united with others which act upon them and are acted upon by them. There is built up as a result a more complex attitude towards the disturbing situations, and this attitude is rendered the more stable in proportion as the combination between the tendencies involved can be made the more perfect.

A REVIEW
& SOME SUGGESTIONS

T‍his book does not pretend to be anything like a complete treatment of the ways in which a study of modern psychology may be of help in the development and maintenance of an efficient army. I have chosen a few interesting and outstanding problems only for discussion. Even these have not been fully dealt with, and there are many others. Practically all the problems which I have discussed have been concerned with ways in which men may be treated, justly and with insight, so as to secure efficiency in the individual and satisfactory organisation in the group, and so as to guard against pathological conditions in both. I have tried to show that psychology may give valuable guidance in determining who is and who is not fit or adapted for the military life; in deciding what the fit person can justly be expected to do well; in training body and mind; in detecting and guarding against undue fatigue; in taking precautions against nervous and mental disorders. I have endeavoured to point out how the study of the determination of conduct in society may yield conclusions which are directly applicable to the maintenance of discipline, to the choice of leaders, to the development of *morale*, and generally to the building up of effective and permanent groups of men.

The mass of important questions which concern how a man may understand and direct the processes leading to his own personal efficiency I have made no attempt to consider. They are at least of equal importance. A man who knows something about the mechanism of the normal processes of perceiving, of remembering and forgetting, of the functions of emotions and the building of sentiments and ideals, of the regulation of bodily and mental activities, inevitably learns much about how to order his life so as to get the best out of himself in the circumstances in which he may be placed.

But even within the rather narrow limits which I have set myself in this book, one fact must force itself upon attention. This is that, concerning every one of the problems which I have treated, the amount that is yet to be learned is very much greater than what can be regarded as established with certainty. Enough is definitely known to be of the greatest practical usefulness, but far more has yet to be discovered.

This very brief review leads to some important conclusions.

First, even as it stands at present, training in psychology should be made a part of any general scheme of preparation for a military career. For this there are three main reasons. There can be no really efficient social organisation unless the individuals concerned are doing the things for which they are most naturally fitted, and are being trained to do these in the most economical ways; it is the direct concern of some of the more technical sides of modern psychology to secure fit training of suitable men. Second, an officer can better handle any group of men if he takes trouble to understand the determination of conduct in and by society ; this is the central problem of modern social psychology. In the third place,—a matter which is of far greater importance than is generally recognised—it is most desirable that any person who takes up a professional career should have some lively interest, outside of the more routine work of his profession, but if possible bearing upon this, which he can prosecute throughout his life. Such an interest, though it be no more than what is called a hobby, is in most cases just what is needed to keep a man keen and alert, to prevent him from stagnating, from falling into hopeless ruts. For a soldier there is nothing better in this way than a study of how human conduct is determined. The materials for this study are to his hand. He is always meeting problems and coming up against difficulties which cannot be met merely by the use of some regular, established convention. Psychology is in fact peculiarly suited to provide a soldier with that interest which is at once a relief from regular duties and an enormous aid to their satisfactory performance.

It is a matter of at least equal importance that adequate facilities should be provided, by military authority, for the prosecution of psychological research. This book has shown that there are already plenty of problems calling for further investigation. These all have their peculiarly military side, and only the soldier who has had both psychological training and practical experience of life in an army can fully appreciate this side.

Two or three instances of problems requiring far more careful psychological investigation than they have yet received may be given. First there is the question of the exact physiological and psychological factors involved in shooting. As I have shown, there has been a strong tendency to lay a great amount of stress upon visual capacities. Within limits this is right, but the other requirements may be of at least as great importance, and very little is definitely established concerning their exact character and the conditions under which they operate. Every special technical branch of army service presents numerous problems of a similar order with regard to the normal reactions of the special senses of vision, hearing, touch and so on, as they are required for military purposes.

Again, as I have shown, very much is yet to be learned as to the most satisfactory methods of teaching skill in movement. Here a particular problem of special interest is that of the significance of the various kinds of reaction-time tests. Perhaps there is no type of psychological experiment that has been more freely and more loosely used for practical purposes than the reaction-time test. Much more needs to be discovered in regard to the exact points and limits of its significance.

Concerning every one of the questions in social psychology which I have discussed in the second part of the book, a vast amount of careful observational work yet remains to be done. Nobody can bring out fully the military importance of this who has not first-hand knowledge of life in an army. I have done little more than define certain problems, for example, of discipline, of leadership, of *morale*, and suggest certain conclusions of practical significance. On all these points much further knowledge should be sought.

But it would be an almost endless task to state, even in general terms, the numerous psychological problems having a bearing upon life in the Army which call for careful and detailed investigation.

It is a matter of immediate practical concern that certain officers who have an aptitude for psychological research, and who have at the same time direct and inside experience of army life, should be encouraged to set to work upon these problems. It is true that modern psychology demands intensive training just as much as chemistry, physics, or engineering, and that a novice is no more likely to be successful in the one than in the others. In the last Great War every belligerent people sooner or later called upon its psychologists for help and advice in regard to numerous specific military and naval problems. Much valuable work was done. Equally it would be true to say that much valuable time was lost and many mistakes were made, because academic methods cannot satisfactorily be applied without modification to special practical conditions. Whether for war or for peace-time organisation, the psychologist who works in the academic laboratory should be asked to train the military officer in methods and theory, and the officer, having the necessary inside practical knowledge, should then apply the methods and theories to his practical problems. The time is ripe for establishing the closest co-operation in research between the laboratory psychologist and the military officer who can be shown to have capacity for psychological work. Any country which undertakes this matter seriously and with judgment will be taking a great step towards rendering its offensive and defensive services efficient in directions which, while they are of supreme importance, have been frequently neglected.

INDEX